CATECHETICS
A Theology of Proclamation

CATECHETICS: A THEOLOGY OF PROCLAMATION is one of the volumes in a new series, IMPACT BOOKS, designed to bring the modern reader the significant achievements of scholars, both Catholic and non-Catholic, in the fields of Scripture, Theology, Philosophy, Mathematics, History, and the Physical and Social Sciences. Among the titles in the series are:

Modern Ethical Theories by James McGlynn, S.J., and Jules Toner, S.J.
The School Examined: An Essay on the Curriculum by Vincent Smith
Catholic Thought in Crisis by Rev. Peter Riga
Contraception and the Natural Law by Germain Grisez
Introducing the Old Testament by Frederick L. Moriarty, S.J.
This Good News: An Introduction to the Catholic Theology of the New Testament by Quentin Quesnell, S.J.
Maturing in Christ: St. Paul's Program for Growth in Christ by George Montague, S.M.
Seven Books of Wisdom by Roland Murphy, O. Carm.
New Testament Essays by Raymond Brown, S.S.
The Word Dwells Among Us by William Lynch, C.M.
God and Contemporary Man by Robert J. Kreyche
With the Eyes of Faith by Rev. John L. Murphy

CATECHETICS

A Theology of Proclamation

BY

REV. ALFRED McBRIDE, O.PRAEM.

ST. NORBERT ABBEY
DE PERE, WISCONSIN

THE BRUCE PUBLISHING COMPANY
MILWAUKEE

268 M

NIHIL OBSTAT:
> Mark A. Steinmetz, O.Praem.

IMPRIMI POTEST:
> Rt. Rev. S. M. Killeen, O.Praem.
> Abbot

NIHIL OBSTAT:
> John A. Schulien, S.T.D.
> Censor librorum

IMPRIMATUR:
> ✠ William E. Cousins
> Archbishop of Milwaukee
> January 6, 1966

Library of Congress Catalog Card Number: 66–16639

© 1966 The Bruce Publishing Company
MADE IN THE UNITED STATES OF AMERICA
(Second printing — 1966)

To
Rt. Rev. S. M. Killeen, O.Praem.
Abbot, Saint Norbert Abbey

Introduction

Who has believed our report? Second Isaiah poses this question before proceeding to recount the cruel passion of the faithful servant of God (Is 53:1 ff.). A catechist is also a reporter who may wonder who believes his report. The position of the catechist is analogous to the men of the prophetic style, who were privileged witnesses to God's action in history, and sufficiently sensitive to the inrush of the Spirit's testimony to realize the awesome significance of these events. The catechist reports godly deeds to the community of believers, hoping to solicit deeper commitment to Jesus, though always aware that the message can meet with resistance and refusal.

The catechist's report must imitate the prophetic response to God's deeds. The prophetic response was not a cool, antiseptic, detached reaction, but an epic, involved, and sagalike declaration. Their testimony to faith is not history in our sense of the term, but saga, in the sense that their memory of the event is the fact plus the total human response to that event. Theirs is a recital of an experience in which God meets man in an intense encounter. It is this sort of testimony which the catechist bears to the world. The catechist's message should have a totality about it, hence it should never be a purely cerebral transmission, nor a pitch for voluntarism, nor an essay in emotional endeavor.

I have tried here to write a series of informal essays on catechetics in the spirit of the ideas just cited. I have limited my contribution mainly to biblical themes which serve as background for the doctrines under discussion. Here and there I have added some liturgical and doctrinal insights which appeared useful and did not overextend the discussion. I have not included any study of the relationship between the personality sciences and the individual doctrines listed, though the first chapter outlines some of the possibilities. This exclusion indicates I have not yet had the opportunity to test the relationships.

I have not intended to present a practical manual of catechetics, because I feel that there is an abundance of pragmatic material available,[1] and that each teacher should develop his or her own structural procedures, proportionate to particular circumstances. Rather, I wish to present some theological perspectives that should hover around each of the doctrines discussed, and to exercise the privilege of prophetic exhortation. Hence the informality of the essays.

The catechist stands at a significant juncture in the evangelizing process. Through him funnel the lofty insights of the research theologian, the exciting world of the biblical scholar, the toneless, objective findings of the personality sciences. The catechist must mediate these to humans, whose variety of social, psychological, and educational patterns and values is almost numbing. This juncture is a cross that can be a glory. I want this book to serve as a shout of encouragement to stay on the firing line until the news sounds so good that nations will bend the knee in joy as they become the eschatological congregations of these latter days, affirming Jesus as Christ and Lord.

---

[1] Cf., for example, Michael Caster, *The Structure of Catechetics* (New York: Herder & Herder, 1965).

Contents

ix

CATECHETICS
A Theology of Proclamation

Chapter 1 ❧ Catechesis:
Its Sources and Communication

I. *The Four Sources of Catechesis*

What is catechetics? It is the transmission of God's message to man for the purpose of evoking commitment and faith in the one to whom we give the message. There are two parts to this description — the announcing of God's message, and the producing, or at least the evoking, of a faith commitment in the person to whom we speak. Catechetics does not exist if one of these elements is absent. The catechist must really be sure that it is God's message which is proclaimed, and retain the intention that somehow the person to whom the message is given will make a commitment to Jesus Christ.

The second element must be done in an atmosphere of freedom. Hence it would be dishonest to transmit God's message with a smile on your face and a club underneath the lectern. Real catechesis occurs in an air of freedom, in a posture of invitation. Such openness is essential to religious growth and religious liberty. If you are going to have God's message, you must be sure you know where to find it. There are four sources of this message: (1) the Bible; (2) Liturgy; (3) Doctrine; (4) Witness. We will now consider each of these in turn.

BIBLE

The biblical revival which we are witnessing today is at the root of all current religious development. It underlines the liturgical renewal, it supports the fresh insights of modern theology, and it is the background for the evangelical fervor so evident in the Church's renewal. Personal witness derives its evangelical flavor and fervor from contact with the word of God.

To view the word of God as a source of catechesis may become easier for you if you see it in terms of its creativity, its dynamism, and its end-time quality. Why do you go to the word of God? First of all because it is creative. What does it create? It creates the Church. This means it creates Christians of those who were not in Christ, and better Christians of those who were.

You know that the Bible is unlike any other book. Do not hold it on an equal level with textbooks in a classroom, and do not treat it the same way you would approach another book. You must by visible witness demonstrate to the students that this book is unique, and that it has a power no other book in existence possesses. Its word thrives with urgency.

God said, "Let there be light," and there was light. Jesus said to a cripple, "Get up and walk," and he walked. Jesus took bread, offered it to His holy remnant in the upper room and said, "This is my body." And it became His body. Peter sent his words out, over Pentecost square, and from those five thousand, isolated, perhaps lonely individuals came a new creation of three thousand Christians.

First of all, the word of God is creative. Never think that any lesson plan you have devised can compare to the word that must be proclaimed from the Bible. Look at Isaiah 55 and compare your own prepared words and ideas about religion to God's consideration of man's thoughts. "For my thoughts are not your thoughts, neither are your ways my ways, says the Lord. For as the heavens are higher than the earth, so are my ways higher than your ways, and my thoughts than your thoughts. For as the rain and the snow come down from heaven, and return not thither but water the earth, making it bring forth and sprout, giving seed to the sower and bread to the eater, so shall my word be that goes forth from my mouth; it shall not return to me empty" (Is 55:8–11).*

It would certainly be a tragedy if the catechist frustrated these words of Isaiah: "It shall not return to me empty." Suppose we have catechists who never even let the word of God be spoken in their classrooms. Suppose we have teachers of religion who never permit the divine rain to come down so that seed be given to the sower and bread to the eater. You can, as catechists, frustrate the creativity of God by refusing to allow His words to be heard in your Christian assembly. If God's word is not heard, then by that token it has not been permitted to exercise its ability to make the Church. But if you utter this word, "Then with joy shall you go out, and in peace shall you be led, and you will not be a thorn in the side of your class. But you shall be like the cypress tree. And the mountains and the hills shall break into singing before you. And the trees of the field will clap their hands. You shall be a memorial to the Lord" (Is 55:12–13).

The word of God creates your class. Read carefully the liturgical constitution and see how it emphasizes the supremacy and superiority of the study of the word of God over all other forms of catechesis. In Germany during World War II, when priests were often forbidden to preach sermons, German bishops petitioned Rome to have the service of the Word in German. The result was that the reading of the word of God in the Fore-Mass became the catechesis for the people. The creative word kept the German Church alive during the war.

Second, this word of God is dynamic. Being dynamic does not mean that you must take this word and shout it at the

---

* All Scripture citations are from *The Bible: An American Translation* by Edgar Goodspeed *et alii*. Copyright, The University of Chicago Press, 1946.

top of your voice, or sweat profusely when you speak, or that you should be a nervous wreck when class is over, so that you need to take pep pills to keep up the pace. The dynamism of the word means that it has within itself the power to change the person who hears it. The old proverb says, "Seeing is believing." But in religion, "Hearing is believing." "Faith comes from hearing," says Paul. Hence modern catechesis stresses the proclamation of the word so that it can be heard. This word must change the listeners.

When Jesus stood on Jordan's bank, He said, "Repent! The kingdom of God is at hand." Repent doesn't mean doing without candy in Lent or giving your body a bad time. Repentance is not spiritual masochism. It is rather *metanoia*, i.e., change. The proclaimed word should make you different. Read Chapter 10 of Matthew's Gospel in which he relates Christ's advice to missionaries. "When you enter a house, say, 'Shalom' (Peace). If the house is worthy, let your peace come upon it; but if it is not worthy, let your peace return to you" (Mt 10:12–13). The uttered word changes the receptive heart, otherwise the word returns to the mouth of the speaker. This whole chapter emphasizes the dynamism of Christ's message. He is out to change people. "Do not think I have come to bring peace on the earth. I have not come to bring peace but the sword" (Mt 10:34).

If you present a message that is so bland and so insipid that you never even provoke opposition, then it is most likely you have not yet arrived at announcing a dynamic word. I do not mean that you should be a controversialist, but your message is of necessity controversial. When you read the Bible to your students, make it sound as though it is speaking to them right now. Do not read the Bible as if it were spoken to someone three thousand years ago. Your students want a word that is up to date, a word that is addressed to their immediate situation. Look now at Jeremiah's opening chapter where we find a theology of the dynamic word.

"Before I formed you in the womb, I knew you, and before you were born, I consecrated you. I appointed you to be a prophet to the nations" (Jer 1:5). These words are meant for every Christian. God tells each member of the people of God, "I have appointed you to be a prophet." What is a prophet? He is not a crystal-ball gazer. Rather he is someone who is so different that when he speaks and acts, people are impelled to turn and look at him. Prophets are extraordinary men, witnesses. How can you be a witness, if you do not draw attention? Jesus said, "Let your light shine before men." The Negro spiritual says, "Let your little light shine." A real prophet is a parousia of Christ, manifesting his Lord in this world. Never in the Church is Christ's parousia more apparent than in the mysterious and delightful moment when you actually find two Christians loving one another. This is the height of prophecy, the supreme expression of Christian witness.

Of course, prophecy involves teaching. You may wish to repeat with Jeremiah, "Ah, Lord God! Behold, I do not know how to speak, for I am only a youth." But God will answer you: "Do not say, 'I am only a youth,' for to all whom I will send you, you shall go, and all that I command you, you shall speak. Be not afraid of them" (Jer 1:6–8). Hence, do not be afraid of your students or your congregation. Don't worry about what they will think, for God is with you to deliver you. You are not out to sell yourself, but to present Jesus Christ. If you accept this assurance of God, you will proclaim a dynamic word. "Then the Lord put forth his hand and touched my mouth; and the Lord said to me, 'Behold, I have put my words into your mouth. See I have set you this day over nations and over kingdoms, to pluck up and break down, to destroy and to overthrow, to build and to plant'" (Jer 1:9–10).

The word is dynamic. You must disintegrate, wreck, ruin, and tear down before you can reintegrate your listeners into the higher synthesis of Christianity. You cannot hope to make your listeners better Christians unless you bring them the dynamic word which can change them. Do not, though, set out to destroy the illusions of your audience unless you are prepared to rebuild them. Karl Barth says we should throw the rock of Scripture into the midst of our students, and then wait. I think there must also be a midwife present to bring the group to a new birth. You must reintegrate your people. That is why God commands Jeremiah "to build and to plant." Imitate Peter at Pentecost. Luke says that Peter's message stung his hearers to the heart, and then Peter went on to build the converts into a Church. This is the dynamic word which changes and creates a new Jerusalem.

Third, the biblical word is eschatological. The Greek word *eschaton* means end-time or final age of the world. We in the Church are living in the end-time, that is, the age in which God's power and will have triumphed in the world. The Church is the long-sought-for messianic age that will last from Jordan's bank until the final cosmic appearance of the Lord. We live now in the last age of man; there will be no other age. How does catechesis reflect this quality of the Church? Suppose you come to class with the Bible in one hand and a paschal candle in the other and joyfully say to your students: "The good news has arrived." This is being eschatological. But, at a deeper level, what are the signs of the end-time? John the presbyter has described them for us in the colorful word of his Apocalypse.

In John's cosmos, four horsemen symbolize the last age of the world. First, a red horse rides into history, coming to take peace away from the earth. He is the sign of war. Next arrives the black horse of famine and hunger, crying in the streets, "Wheat at a dollar a quart, barley at three quarts for a dollar" (Ap 6:6). Then comes a pale horse whose rider's name is Death. These unholy three are commissioned to dominate a fourth of the earth, killing with the sword, famine, and plague. Our own age has seen these grim riders.

The murder of six million Jews and the slaughter of sixty million others in the wars of this century are evident and painful reminders that the pale horse of death and red horse of war witness the end-time. Demographers project that a frightful famine may strike the world by 1974, grapes of wrath that would make Steinbeck shudder. The black horse of famine witnesses for us the end-time.

If our world is in agony, should there not be some sign of redemption? There is. "Then I saw heaven opened, and behold, a white horse! He who sat upon it is called faithful and true. He judges and wages war in righteousness. His eyes blaze like fire. . . . He is clad in a robe dipped in blood and the name by which he is called is the Word of God" (Ap 19:11–13).

The Rider on the white horse lives in a real world where there is mud, tears, sweat, and blood. He is the sign of hope in the midst of war, hunger, and death, and His name is the Word of God, which is the principal source of catechesis. Follow this mysterious Horseman who will shepherd you with His staff of iron. He will make the sword of judgment come from your mouth, that like Jesus you will be a sign of contradiction to your generation.

Armed with the word of God you will bring salvation or judgment to your classrooms and pulpits; you will present a Christianity of challenge. On the clothing and thigh of the Rider of the white horse is written: King of Kings and Lord of Lords. Hence the basic proclamation of catechesis is Jesus Christ. You are not communicating pieces of paper but the person of your Savior; you must proclaim *Him*, not *it*. The only reason our Lord needs catechists is to bring a person to the word. Poor catechesis is applying a book to a student. Rich catechesis is bringing the warmth of your own person as faithful and true to Jesus to the message of the Bible.

The word of God remains as the basic and primary source of your catechesis and the thrust for your evangelical fervor

that will aid you to make the gospel a sign of joy and redemption to the children of this generation.

LITURGY

Do not look upon liturgy merely as rubrics. Rubrics refer
to the red print in the missals, but liturgy is not simply
mechanics. We are not producing sacred mechanisms, but
trying to evoke from the people of God an authentic religious experience. Liturgy is not so much the official prayer
of the Church as it is the official presence of God. Liturgy
is the holy ground where the Christian should experience
his God.

Liturgy should be the peak experience of faith. It should
be the ultimate goal of catechesis to bring your students to
meet their God in the liturgical event. If you have a catechesis
that merely produces very bright people, and perhaps decent
citizens, but has never brought them to meet God, then
your catechesis has failed. Catechesis is meant to lead to
commitment and faith. This occurs mainly in the official
salvation event which we call liturgy. You can read the
Bible; you can study the Bible; but unless you celebrate the
Bible in a liturgical event, its evangelical power can be lost.
In liturgy you are initiated into an experience of God. I
do not use the word "experience" in a cheap and grossly
emotional fashion, but rather as the total, personal involvement of the Christian with his redeemer.

It is entry into God that I plead for. I realize that this
is obscure and that it is the realm of darkest faith and that
no catechist can manipulate his students into such an experience. But a catechist can so train the student, so situate
him, that if he has any sense of openness and surrender, he
will come to know his Lord.

The liturgy is both word and sacrament, and as word it
has a highly important catechetical value. The liturgy of
the word contains readings from the Bible and a sermon.
Its purpose is to continue the work of evangelization, to

imitate Peter and sting the hearts of the assembled people to open their hearts to the sacrament. See the sacraments as recurrences of Christ's redeeming action in time.

In the early Church, the liturgy was, by and large, the only source of catechesis. We cannot return to that blissful age, but the emergence of a vernacular liturgy in our times reopens its catechetical possibilities. From Advent to Pentecost the Church recites the major mysteries of the life of Jesus. It is not possible in any one liturgical event to get our minds around the whole mystery of Jesus. Our minds are simply too small. It would be wonderful if we could proclaim the whole message in one word. Only one person could do that — our Father in heaven who did utter the whole message in one word, the divine *logos*, Jesus. You and I, because of our fallible and finite intellects, and the weakness of our comprehension, must receive the word in the variety of images and words which the liturgy spaces out over the Church year. Through the course of the Church year we may contemplate the fullness of the mystery of Jesus who comes to save us.

When you are using the liturgy as a source of catechesis, tell your students that the Lord who acts that day does so under the particular aspects of the day's mystery. If it is the feast of the Transfiguration, then the Lord they will know is the Christ of light and glory, who illumines those who sit in darkness, who transfigures every poor human being from the lowliness of this body into the glory of the resurrection.

Liturgy is a source of catechesis bringing the dead word to life by the official encounter of Christians with God.

DOCTRINE

Between the Bible and the student there needs to be a bridge, something to make the biblical events relevant to them. It is the role of doctrine to build this bridge. The great cry of Church renewal is relevancy. Through doctrine we look at the diverse elements of Sacred Scripture, abstract from the sometimes contradictory and heavily detailed data, and produce a detached and clear idea. If Scripture is concrete and historical, doctrine is abstract and systematic. Some today want to abandon the systematic approach and plead that abstraction ought not to interfere with catechesis. This is an exaggeration. We need the biblical approach and the systematic theological efforts too. Doctrine helps us to relate the ancient words of the Bible to the culture of our times.

Words grow tired, just as blood becomes tired and needs medicine. Religious words grow tired for two reasons. First, because of the nature of language. In each generation language undergoes a transformation and upheaval. Who today besides some specialist understands the English of Chaucer?

A second reason why words grow tired is the very ambiguity of religion itself. Religion is paradoxical. For example, "world" in John's Gospel is a bad word, but in the Book of Genesis, it is a good word. "God saw the world, and he saw that it was good." John says that the world is the home of the prince of darkness and the source of evil. What are you going to think about the world? Is it good or is it bad? It's both. That is what I mean by ambiguity and paradox in religion. To experience ambiguity you must place yourself in the midst of the opposing ideas and feel the tension this produces. You remain there blending the contradictory forces until a temporary synthesis is reached.

In turn you will reexperience tension on a new level and go on to another synthesis. This is what gives you your penetration of religious truth. There is nothing new about this. Theologians have always wrestled with the dilemmas of religious mysteries in their attempts to gain new insight. Ambiguity is uncomfortable, hence a cultural prejudice can shift theology to favor one or another horn of the dilemma. The post-Reformation Church retreated somewhat from involvement in the affairs of the world. This produced a monasticlike quality in the Church that had the unwitting result of evoking hostility to the world.

Theological words grow tired because of the ambiguity of religion and the natural weariness of the human frame. Because this is so, each generation must rethink old truths. New theology is not new truths, but a fresh restatement of the old ones. You may present a religious formula to your students and insist it be accepted because it is true, but this is insufficient. It is not enough to be true, it must also seem true, be felt as fact. Everyone is looking for the truth but the problem is to present the discovered truth in such a way that it sounds like truth. In law courts men thirst for justice, but the decision of the judge must not only be just, it must seem just.

In the area of doctrine, catechists face a theological lag, inasmuch as the doctrinal theologians have not yet been able to produce a manageable synthesis of the explosion in biblical and liturgical studies. Hence catechists must be patient until our theologians can catch up.

WITNESS

Personal witness is the fourth source of God's message. I think you must realize that today people are not out to listen to you so much as to look at you. They are less concerned with what you are saying than with what you are doing. If you do not appear as someone thoroughly convinced of your message, it is quite likely you will be rejected or ignored. In our times, more than in any other, the catechist must be prophetic. You must make your audience squirm at times, and be inflamed with the message you are giving. Jesus says: "I have come to set fire to the earth." Yet many religion classrooms look like dying embers and many Sunday congregations are as dry as ashes.

We must restore the flame of Christianity, and remember that this fire does not exist in books. It exists in people.

It is only in personal relation, in the restoration of personal witness that we can reconvince the people of our age of the importance of Christianity. As a catechist you have a unique role to play. You stand between the student and God, and you are all he has. Generally there is no other way whereby the student will meet his God. How can he know the Father unless he sees the Father shining through you?

You must no longer hide your light under a bushel; you must be a city set on a hill. You must be the salt of your classroom and the light of your students. You must be a living light. Such is personal witness. Since I will devote a full chapter to this idea later on, no more is needed here.

SUMMARY

If you intend to communicate God's message then you must use all four sources cited above. Do not ignore any of them. If you think that only the Bible is needed for catechesis then you will fall into the error of biblicism. You will train clever students who know much about form criticism, but perhaps little about Christianity. If you use only the liturgy, you can produce litniks grossly concerned about an ever so pious act in the parish church, but who would not lift their fingers to help a Negro; in short, your students would not see any relationship between liturgy and life.

If you use only doctrine, you will produce people with refined and abstract mentalities, but whose actions are as irrelevant as their mental outlooks. Abstraction alone is not enough. You will seldom move anyone's heart with an abstraction. And if you are not out to move someone's heart, then you are not a catechist. God tells us in Jeremiah 31:31: "I will write a new law on the heart of man."

If you employ only witness as a source for catechesis, then you will produce fanatics, people all fired up about religion, but without intellectual content or biblical data or doctrinal basis. These people constitute the lunatic fringe and plague every new movement. Note that fanatics generally ignore one or another of the sources we have mentioned.

Hence your task is far from simple. You must employ all these sources always, arranging them in an attractive and balanced order. Feel at home with the Bible (all of it), and at ease with the highly symbolic language and gesture of the liturgy. Read contemporary doctrine for a fresh formulation of the old truths. Witness conviction in proclaiming your message.

II. Catechesis: A Message Communicated to Man

Not only do you bring God's message, but you must bring it to man. This means you must know something about man. Take advantage of the modern sciences which help us to gain a deeper knowledge of man's motivations and drives. Know his psychology, sociology, and the prevailing winds of doctrine which have made an impact on him.

Psychology. Since education is a communication between persons, it is imperative to have a clear idea of the psychology of the student you teach. When you prepare a lesson on baptism, don't say: "What ideas should I give the student on baptism?" Rather say: "What ideas do the students already have about baptism?" Begin with the student, not your own ideas. High school freshmen may be more disposed to the fact-finding approach (global), while sophomores and juniors caught up in their interior crises are absorbed in self-discovery (analytic), and the seniors are getting ready to assume their social role in the world (synthetic). Tailor your teaching to these potentialities in your student.

Sociology. Have a general awareness of the type of homes and neighborhoods from which your students come. How would you teach divorce to a boy whose parents are divorced? How would you teach Sunday worship to a boy whose older brothers and father never worship on Sunday? How do you reconcile conflicting moralities — the one taught at school and the one experienced in the home? How do you handle students who come from homes in which there is no cultural awareness at all, no encyclopedias or world books, no LP classics, a home in which the parents never read? Will not such situations influence the response your student can give?

Modern Attitudes. Remember the modern world is *dynamic;* it has little patience with the static. Your students live in homes stacked with magazines about racing cars, and piles of records that issue music played so fast the singers can scarcely breathe. The students live in a world of speed and movement. When they come to class they expect to find in religion the same movement and excitement, the same sense of dynamism. In their world power is pushing rockets into the skies. If you give them a bland religion, in the face of these magnificent and beautiful achievements of man, they will not buy it.

If they watch the Saturn rocket taking off on its way to the moon, then come and hear you discourse on God's immutability, they may wonder, "What has this got to do with me?" They live in a dynamic world that is on the move. If you teach the gifts of the Holy Spirit as little boxes placed in the soul, which, like Pandora's case, can occasionally be opened to let some power out, instead of teaching them that the gifts are signs of the powerful presence of the Spirit driving them to be true Christian witnesses, then you are out of tune with the dynamic approach of our times. A modern youth can understand the Spirit's presence; he knows what it means to feel an impulse, to be under pressure. Tell him about the pressure of the Spirit which can drive him to be saved and to help save others.

Personalism. The drive for personalism is everywhere apparent today. It is a reaction against the impersonalism of our age. Automation, mass education, mass media, and mass taste project people into a state of loneliness. It puts them on islands, and like anyone stranded on an island they want to be rescued. They are experiencing what we call alienation.

They are not functioning as persons so much as zip codes, numbers, and more numbers. What they want to hear from you is this assurance: "I know you. You are a person, who may be lost and alone, who lives in a world of fantasy and wants to be real. I know you have been running so that you can forget your loneliness. Today, I bring you the Person of Jesus Christ, who loves you, who wants you, and who saves you."

In your catechesis present a personal savior to an audience scarred by impersonalism. Don't say, "Baptism is the sacrament which . . ." Rather, "Baptism is the great event in which Jesus brought you into His assembly of the redeemed. . . ." Don't treat commandments as paper laws; present them as signs of love that show gratitude to God for His saving work.

Summary

The catechist stands between God's message and man, as a prophetic mediator between the two. The program is three-fold: to inform, to form, and to initiate. It is initiation that makes catechesis a religious event, for by it the student is led to experience God and make the act of faith-surrender. As catechist you must draw on the four sources of God's message, know the psychology and sociology of your audience, and incorporate the dynamism and personalism of our culture into your thinking, blending all these elements into a workable presentation. You do not act alone, for Christ is actively present in you, uttering His creative and dynamic word. Let Him have His way.

Chapter 2 ❧ God, Our Father

Ordinarily God the Father is taught in terms of His qualities. We say that He is all-perfect, immutable, all-knowing.
This is telling what God *is*. I think we should present God
in the context of what He does more than what He is. Be
more concerned with His doing than with His being. Be an
existentialist here rather than an essentialist. Telling the student only about God's qualities gives too static a picture.

The Bible gradually unfolds the idea of God our Father.
Among the Hebrews and early Christians when children
were asked "Who is God?" they would not speak of Him
as Creator so much as Savior. They would say that God is
the One who led their forefathers out of the land of slavery
into the terrain of freedom. The creed of a Jewish boy would
be to announce his faith in a God who redeems. The basic
catechetical notion about God in Jewish catechesis was that
God is Savior.

Religious realities arrange themselves in a hierarchy, at the
summit of which is the Father. If we have been remiss in
situating the Father properly, we must not be so now. He is
fundamental to our catechetical work, for it is to the Father
that we are sending the child.

God as Redeemer is the basic revelation, not God as
Creator. The opening chapters of Genesis which describe
God as creator are later additions to Scripture. These chapters
resulted perhaps from the experience of the exile in Babylon
when the Jewish community was confronted with the creation tales of the local religions. These wild stories from the
Babylonian myths were repellent to the Jews, who then
sought to counter them with a divinely inspired view of crea-

tion. Under the Spirit's impulse the prophetic community fashioned a purified narrative, putting it where it logically belonged, at the beginning of the canon of sacred books.

The Father first appears historically on the plains of Haran where, in some mysterious and unexplainable way, He encounters the pilgrim Abram. The very name of this man is significant, for the prefix Ab means "Father," hence the father meets the Father. The first confrontation and the ones which follow gradually reveal the meaning of our Father. The special revelation about our Father in the Abram story is that He is Redeemer. God tells Abram that he will have a son, from whom will come a nation, and in that nation all others will be blessed. From this favored people shall come redemption for the rest of the world. After all, why did God make this nation, but that they might be the light of all the other peoples. The word "bless" in the Bible does not mean Sign of the Cross, but the self-giving of the Father, the outpouring of His life. Blessing is a transmission of life. Now the Father's own life will flow into history. Ultimately this life will come to men through a death-life action. The Abram story provides a dress rehearsal for this event.

Abram, given the name Abraham, is instructed to take his only son and sacrifice him on Mt. Moriah. The "only son" text would be later applied to the relation between God and Jesus. As you know, God did not demand the actual death of Isaac. This young lad asked his father, "Who shall provide the lamb?" Abraham answered prophetically, "God shall give us the lamb." On Jordan's bank, John the Baptist pointed at Jesus and declared Him to be the Lamb who takes away the sins of the world. What is symbolically acted at Moriah becomes a reality at Calvary when the Father gives His son for the sake of saving us from sin. The Father's intention is to save.

The early books of the Bible show the Father as living close to His people. He dines in the tent of Abraham. Jacob, the crafty son of Isaac, paces the fields of Peniel one night, deeply troubled because his uncle Laban is coming from the north in anger against him, and his brother Esau is riding from the south with four hundred wild Arabs to punish him for stealing the birthright. God the Father comes to this lonely, troubled man, and, in the form of an angel, wrestles with him. Here the Father struggles for the conscience and soul of man, until Jacob surrenders and God makes this man Israel, "the man who prevailed with God" (Gn 32:39).

God has shown Himself as immanent, close to His people. But then He wishes to reveal another side to His presence, namely, His transcendence. One day Moses trudges up the heights of Sinai, and God appears to him in the burning bush. Now Moses does not dine with God; there is no wrestling scene. The Father tells Moses to stand back, take off his shoes, and approach with fear (cf. Ex 3). This fear means awe and reverence, not terror. God tells Moses that he stands on holy ground. The word "holy" means that which is separated from the profane. God here introduces a new note in the divine catechesis, by insisting on separation, and commanding Moses not to come closer. This teaches the otherness of God, His majesty and glory, before whom Moses hides his face in fear.

Now God becomes someone wondrous, burning. In a column of fire He leads His people out of Egypt. God comes as a mighty wind which moves aside the waters of the sea, so impressing the people with His power. If you want to speak of the omnipotence of God do it the way the Bible does, by telling a story. Read to your students the great text about the victory at the Reed Sea in Exodus 14.

"The Lord said to Moses, 'Why do you cry to me. Tell the people of Israel to go forward. Lift up your rod, and stretch out your hand over the sea and divide it, that Israel may go on dry land through the sea.' And the Lord drove the sea back, by a strong east wind all night, and made the sea dry land. And in the morning watch, the Lord in the

pillar of fire and of the cloud looked down upon the host
of the Egyptians and discomfited them, clogging their chariot
wheels so that they drove heavily. . . . And the Lord routed
the Egyptians in the midst of the sea" (Ex 14:15–16, 24–25,
27). This is our Father, a God of action, no longer the
family intimate of the patriarchal days, but now a divinity
of splendor and might, the holy God.

The prophets complete this theology of transcendence. The
best example is the vision of Isaiah in Chapter 6 of his book.

In the year that King Oziah died, the young aristocrat
Isaiah went to the temple for an elaborate liturgy. Because
of his privileged position in society he was shown to one
of the front seats. There he sat immersed in the atmosphere
of gold and purple vestments, clouds of sweet incense,
rhythmic ascendancies of chant and the stately paces of
liturgical movement.

Then, caught up in the measured ecstasy of the celebration, he is lifted up by the Lord to a vision. As the prophet
looked toward the thick darkness of the room called the
holy of holies, the house of the ark, he noted the present
liturgy of earth giving way to the liturgy of heaven.

He sees the Lord high and uplifted on a throne, much
as the cloud has rested on the ark at times. The skirts of
God's robe filled the temple, meaning that the awesome
presence of God penetrated the whole place, as close as the
feeling of cloth against the skin. The servants of the throne
are seraphim, fire angels. The angels use two of their six
wings to cover their faces, symbolizing the mystery of God's
otherness, just as the masked face evokes mystery and terror.
No one may see God's face and live. Isaiah hears about God's
holiness from a song which the angels chant, as later shepherds would hear angels sing of Jesus' glory on the hill-
sides of Bethlehem. Whenever the silence of heaven is
broken, we hear the song of God's holiness and glory.

This idea of the holy expresses that quality which is opposed to sin. Rudolph Otto says that our experience of holi-

ness is an ambiguous reaction of fear and fascination. Moses on the holy ground takes off his shoes and fearfully huddles close to the earth, yet remains fascinated by the bush that burns without being consumed. Peter, James, and John on the mount of the transfiguration react similarly before the burning glory of Christ.

Then the foundations of the temple threshold began to shake. As thunder, lightning, and the roar of the sea helped primitive man understand the might of God, so here Isaiah knows the almighty Father. Then the vision blacks out in a cloud of smoke. Isaiah stands dazed and alone, aware of himself in contrast to what he has seen. In his weak and sinful condition he has confronted the matchless holiness and glory of God.

His position is similar to a man naked before God at the judgment moment of death. Isaiah looks into his heart and, after making an examination of conscience, utters the anguished admission, "Woe is me, for I am lost. I am a man of unclean lips" (Is 6:5). He asserts that the reason for this is due to his vision of the Lord of hosts.

Next the cloud vanishes and the vision reappears. A fiery angel takes a hot coal from the altar of incense and presses it against the unclean lips of the prophet and recites a kind of sacramental formula over him: "Behold this has touched your lips; your guilt is taken away, and your sin forgiven" (Is 6:7). The fire is both a purification and salvation symbol. It is not merely the lips of the prophet which rejoiced in purification, it is the person of Isaiah himself, bathed in God's fire.

God speaks, "Whom shall I send, and who will go for us?" (Is 6:8.) The Father has a mission for the prophet. God, however, respects his freedom. The purified Isaiah, evaluating his elevated condition, having a new heart forged by divine courage, looks into the face of God and says, "Here am I! Send me" (Is 6:8).

Notice the movement of the vision. God first advances upon the prophet, breaking into his prayerful reverie at a liturgical function. The acts of Isaiah are a response resulting from an awareness of the divine initiative. God speaks to him with a vision of His unapproachable glory and holiness. Isaiah responds with an admission of his unworthy sinfulness. God speaks again with the purifying fire of the seraph along with a call to apostolic mission. Isaiah makes a response of repentance and love.

This splendid vision describes the Father as the holy one, that is, a God of unspeakable glory, totally other from man, high and uplifted. This revelation helps us to understand what sin means as a condition completely opposed to the holiness of our Father.

The next period to deepen our knowledge of the Father was the age of wisdom in which the post exilic community of faith felt the need to have a strong interior life and meet our Father in contemplation. This is a time of silence. The epic sagas of Judges and Kings and the fiery speeches of the great prophets no longer shake the bones of Israel. Only the quiet aphorisms of the wisdom writers and the prayerful spirit of the community of the just appear. The mystery of our Father is so great we stand mute before it, and await a new burst, a new utterance, which is Jesus our Lord.

This development of the biblical notion of our Father recalls the need to affirm that such religious ideas are mysteries. This means that it will not be possible to give a totally clear idea of the Father. The biblical account is ambivalent; it has the ambiguity of paradox. God is first seen as a friendly intimate, and later as the distant clean God of majesty enthroned. He holds man by the hands and then draws back into the thick darkness of the holy. Such a God we must proclaim, hoping that the apparent contradictions will not be frustrating, but rather a challenge to contemplation, the work of faith.

The New Testament states that Jesus Himself is the revelation of His Father. "Phillip said to Jesus, 'Lord, show us the Father and we shall be satisfied.' Jesus said to him,

'Have I been with you so long and yet you do not know me, Phillip? He who has seen me has seen the Father' " (Jn 14:9). When the Church contemplates Jesus as the manifestation of our Father, it gains an insight into its vocation. The doctrine of Father becomes one of the principal searchlights that help the Church know the spectrum of Christian mystery.

Jesus is related to His Father in terms of knowledge and love. Jesus does things only His Father could do, namely, He raises the dead, controls storms and pronounces judgment on sin. He does not accomplish this simply because He knows the Father but because He and the Father are one in love. The Father endows Jesus with full authority and glorifies His son. Jesus stands in history as the sole mediator of the Father. The intimacy declared to exist between Father and Son is the model of the knowledge which must exist between the Son and the Apostles. The community of knowledge and love abiding between Father and Son extends to a community of knowledge between Son and disciples.

The illumination of the Father-Son relationship helps us know the meaning of Christ. It also helps know the meaning of the Church. God is the Father of the members of the Church because He is the Father of Jesus. Like Christ, the Church must reproduce the activity of the Father, becoming as perfect as He is. The Father and Jesus confer the Holy Spirit upon the Church, which must mediate God to the world. "Let your light so shine before men, that they may see your good works, and give glory to your Father who is in heaven" (Mt 5:16).

The New Testament Church sometimes used the word "child" for "Christian." One reason why is that Christ took a child in His arms one day and told men that they needed to become like a child to enter His Church. Entering the Church meant assuming a filial relationship to the Father. Jesus dedicated Himself to death in order to gather together the children of God scattered abroad, and declared that the divine mysteries were hidden from the wise and prudent, but made known to the children (cf. Lk 10:21).

Another New Testament name for Christian is brother. In the Acts of the Apostles and the Epistle to the Romans the word "brother" is used for Jews twelve times, and for Christians one hundred and seventy-four times. Men who enter the Church are no longer strangers or slaves, but beloved brothers. Jesus was the firstborn of many brothers, hence His insistence on brotherly reconciliation before worship. Paul deeply lamented the controversy among the brothers at Corinth (cf. 1 Cor 6:5). John flatly stated that no man can love God unless he loves his brother (cf. 1 Jn 4:20).

Liturgy

Liturgy celebrates our sonship and the fatherhood of God, joyfully declaring our divine adoption. Liturgical gatherings proclaim the mighty deeds of our Father, leading us to an encounter with Him. With few exceptions, every oration is addressed to the Father. Yet, since we cannot call Him Father unless we are identified with Jesus, the whole movement of liturgy is always through Christ our Lord.

Liturgy is the mirror of our faith, reflecting what we believe through song, prayer, gesture, and sacrament. As Abraham capitulated in faith at Mount Moriah, as Moses took the tables of the law at Sinai, as the young Church was born in the upper room, so on the holy mount of the liturgy, the Christian touches the peak experience of faith.

Because liturgy demands a community of those who acknowledge that Jesus is the Lord, the brotherhood of Christians for whom Christ died and rose must be conscious of who they are. There is no Father without a Son, and all at the liturgy who admit their sonship must also admit their brotherly relationship to the rest of the worshipers. The communal demand of the liturgy is a constant reminder of our sonship in Christ, of our brotherhood in Him as sons of the heavenly Father. The community-minded prayers and the call for common action plus the challenge to love make the liturgy a dramatic reminder of the true meaning of our Christian existence.

Doctrine

We turn to the Apostles' Creed for a doctrinal approach to the Father. "I believe in God the Father almighty, the creator of heaven and earth." So many catechists teach the creed as an abstract doctrine, whereas originally it was considered a recital of the major works of the history of salvation. The creed, then, is not so much a recitation of doctrine as of historical deeds. Today we call this a theology of proclamation.

This Christian creed, as does the Bible, begins with the declaration that God is Father-Creator. Being Father means creator, as He brings us into being by the outpouring of His love. The creed then shows God as Savior through His work of creation, not just the first one which saw the world come into being, but also the new creation described by John in his prologue where the Father is the Author of the *Logos* in whom appears the new creation that saves mankind.

Hence it is best to link intellectually and emotionally redemption with creation and then both in turn with the Father. To this add the idea that the Father is the Source of all authority. Do not, however, describe the authority of the Father in terms of a secular totalitarian political form. Divine authority is *authorship*, and God's authority is that of loving creation — redemption, not the dominance of a tyrant. God is the author of all reality. He authors us. In a catechetics class, your authority imitates God as you create and produce citizens of the Church.

You are familiar with the phenomenon of language known as word association, in which one word immediately calls to mind several others. One word association chain you should have is this: Father-creator-redeemer-authority. By approaching the doctrine of God the Father in this manner you will

be helped in evading one pitfall, namely the obstacle presented by the child's human father. Psychiatry shows that the
human father can sometimes obstruct your catechesis of God
the Father, though, admittedly it can also be a great help.
When you use the word "father" with a child, he naturally
will think of dad.

But if the child's father is a severe and cruel man, how
will you teach God as the loving Creator and Redeemer? I
am not perfectly sure how this barrier can be overcome, but
I do suggest keeping the emphasis on the biblical notion sup-
ported by liturgical celebration.

Psalm 103 has an especially beautiful view of God the
Creator. The psalmist pierces the naturalness of things to
affirm his faith in his Creator. The Father's chambers are
above the waters, and the clouds are His chariot. Winds are
His voice and the lightning, His servant. Springs flash up
at His command, and mountain streams flow from His
chambers. The Father plants grass and the wheat of the field,
the vines on the hills so that men may have bread and heart-
warming wine. He plants trees for the birds and appoints a
moon for the seasons. He gives night to the roving beasts
and prey to the roaring lion. And all this He did with wisdom.
Every man and beast looks to God in due season, and shudders
on the day that God hides His face.

The Father has now given wheat and wine the glory of
being sacrament. He has made oil and water mix for the
baptism of water and the Spirit. The old heaven and earth
have passed away and are supplanted by the new. It is the
kingdom of His beloved Son, Jesus. The Church children of
our Father sing to Him and serve Him with gladness.

It is good to see our Father in His abiding posture of
Creator. As He once sent His Spirit over the chaos in Genesis
and brought forth life, so today His breath sweeps through
the earth. This is the reason why the Church prays: "Send
forth your Spirit and create anew the face of the earth."
Each dawn heralds the creation of new brothers in Jesus,

born by the power of the Father working through the Son in the Spirit.

Witness

The committed Christian knows how to put first things first. To him the basic memory is that of God our Father. The enthusiasm of the fervent Christian flows from his deep attachment to the primeval revelation of God as Father who creates and saves His people through His Son, Jesus. Today the Christian cannot afford to touch religion lightly or esoterically. This is not the time for "hold-the-line indifference," nor for the thin diet of academic disclosure. "I will go to my Father's house" is the cry of the modern Christian who decides to evidence religion in all he says and does.

Summary

The Bible shows the Father as Savior of His people, who reveals Himself gradually to them in the paradox of immanence and transcendence. They eventually see Him as Creator as well, making not only the cosmos but also the new creation which is the Church. Liturgy emphasizes that the Father is the goal of worship and of all Christian existence. Doctrine, taking its cue from the theology of recital in the Apostles' Creed, teaches a Father of action who authors existence. Witness remembers that all Christian energy flows from the basic affirmation about God's fatherhood.

There is nothing exhaustive about these words; they are signs pointing to the rich catechetical possibilities resident in the renewed theological disciplines.

Chapter 3 ✤ Jesus Our Savior

What does the Bible say about Jesus? It proclaims Him as the central figure of the history of salvation. If you wish to teach the meaning of Jesus, you must know the Old Testament. If Jesus proclaims the good news, you must know something about the bad news. Not that the Old Testament is a chronicle of dreary tales and bad news, for it is a story of great beauty, but approach it to find out why we needed Christ. Do not begin in medias res, for Jesus should be understood against His background. The New Testament writers were culturally Old Testament men, speaking, thinking, and acting in the image patterns and traditions of Israel. Hence, to teach Jesus, you must teach the Old Testament preparation for His coming.

The Bible tells us that Jesus is the great sacrament. It does not use that word, but conveys that idea. We are constricted by a narrower idea of sacrament, employing it technically for the seven sacraments. But the word has a broader connotation. Jesus, as portrayed in the New Testament, was the revelation and effective action of God. You find no record, for example, of Jesus baptizing His Apostles. There is no indication that He had to do this, for Jesus Himself was present to them. He bodied Himself over against them and affected them as a person affects a person. The reason we have sacraments is to provide the holy ground whereon two persons can meet. Sacraments are not things, but are situations, acts, whereby man can meet Jesus and submit to His saving action.

Jesus was the sacrament of His own time. He was, as John says, the sign to His generation. This is clear in the

27

case of the cure of the paralytic, who was lowered through the roof. He is brought to Jesus for the purpose of being cured. Jesus turns to the man, and in the warmth of His voice and the power of His presence pronounces an absolution: "Son, your sins are forgiven." Perhaps the man was disappointed. We don't know. We do know that Jesus does not say right away: "Now, I'll cure you." In fact Jesus turns away from the cripple and enters into a debate with the Pharisees on the other side of the room. They argue about Christ's ability to forgive sins. Nothing is said about curing the man. They knew that He could cure the man; they denied that He could forgive the man's sins.

When Jesus presents the challenge, "Don't you think I can forgive this man's sins?" the only man in that crowded, dusty room who could give the true answer is the one who had experienced the sacrament of Christ's presence. The only man who knew that Jesus could indeed forgive sins was the man who had been confronted with the personal presence of God and was shaken inwardly by a mysterious tranquillity, an inner realization of rightness that he experienced when he knew he was reconciled to God.

Jesus was the sacrament of salvation to His time, and He remains as such for our age as well.

It has long been customary to teach the "Life of Jesus," but this was not, as modern biblical scholars point out, the intention of the Gospel writers. Their great concern was to proclaim a list of events linked theologically for the purpose of converting the hearers to Jesus. When you proclaim Jesus and the events of His life, do this as the Gospels did. The early Christian preachers and teachers used a four-point outline in their presentation of Jesus. They began with His baptism, then spoke of His Galilean ministry, followed this with the account of His journey to Jerusalem, and concluded with the passion-resurrection narrative at Jerusalem.

Build your catechesis of Jesus around this outline. This

was the way He proclaimed Himself through the inspiration
of the sacred writers. This is Christ's own self-revelation as
canonized by the Sacred Books. If you want to have as real
and authentic catechesis as possible, then follow the original
evangelical procedure as outlined in the Gospels.

The Baptism. When Jesus goes to the Jordan to be baptized by John, He does so for His messianic investiture. The
event is sacramental in tone. He walks into the water and
His father recites a formula over Him: "This is my beloved
son, with whom I am well pleased" (Mt 3:17). This bap-
tismal-like formula is an echo of two Old Testament texts:
Psalm 2:7 and Isaiah 42:1-4. The quote from Psalm 2 shows
that Jesus is the crown prince of David's house come to save
the people. The citation from Isaiah declares that Jesus will
be a suffering Messiah. Both texts confirm Jesus as the Savior,
whether royal or suffering. Isaiah 42:1 states: "Behold my
servant whom I uphold, my chosen, in whom my soul de-
lights. I have put my Spirit upon him, he will bring forth
justice to the nations." To bring justice does not simply mean
that He will produce equality between rich and poor, though
He will indeed have a care for social justice.

The basic meaning of bringing justice is transmitting
salvation. To bring justice is to make a man just. Jesus is
the Savior. In teaching the baptismal sequence, include the
stories about the Baptist and the temptation event which
follows the Jordan scene.

Galilean Ministry. The Galilean ministry is in large part
a story of the miracles of Jesus. When you teach the miracles
do not concentrate on their philanthropic aspect. Don't
produce a Ben Casey or Doctor Kildare atmosphere, pictur-
ing Jesus as having the ideal bedside manner. This is not
the main point. True enough, Jesus is a very kind Man,
moved with sorrow by the misery of men, compassionately
reaching out to heal and console. But the main reason why
Jesus performs miracles is to save. Recall the story of the

paralytic in which the cure comes as a sort of afterthought. Christ was more concerned to deliver this man from sin than to give him the power to walk.

Teach the miracles as prototypes of the sacraments and evangelical pronouncements. Today's miracles are the saving events of the Church. The mighty deeds in the desert by the God of the Exodus, the marvelous works of Jesus in Galilee continue today in the evangelical and sacramental system. This does not exclude the extraordinary charismatic events at places like Lourdes and Fatima, which are divine gifts meant to give a lively and specialized witness of the abundance of God's power and love. But the biblical miracles are less this sort of witness and more the mighty action of God continued constantly and universally in history. In Galilee, Jesus in His miracles stands as Savior.

The Journey to Jerusalem. Read Luke 9:51: "When the days drew near for him to be received up, he set his face to go to Jerusalem." The "receiving up" text refers to both the lifting up of Jesus on the cross and His exaltation at the right hand of the Father. He sets His face toward Jerusalem and begins the paschal journey to the holy city. The nine chapters which Luke devotes to this trip are called the "travel document of Luke." It is not simply a geographical narrative, but a story of Christ's paschal journey to Jerusalem for the newer and greater Exodus. The whole journey is in terms of salvation.

Along the way Jesus tells many *parables.* His main purpose is not just to catch the ear of the uninstructed listener with a fascinating tale. He did not tell the parables simply to satisfy a pedagogical need of people too uneducated to grasp abstract ideas. Nor is His intention a purely obvious attempt at the morality fable. Christ's principal reason for telling the parables was to announce the arrival of God's reign on earth. The parable is told, not for its moral exhortation — though this is not absent completely — but primarily to declare that the kingdom of God is here. The pearl, the leaven, the mustard seed, the wedding banquet, the rich man and Lazarus are wonderful stories of a kingdom arrived here and now.

If they were only moral homilies, then it is unlikely that Jesus would say so insistently: "Don't you understand? . . . Let him who has ears, let him hear. . . . To you it is given to know the mysteries of the kingdom of God, to the rest in parables" (Mt 13:9, 11–14).

What Jesus means is that two kinds of people hear His parables, but only those who with faith have accepted the kingdom understand what they mean. The parable is a mystery of God's election sorting out the saved from the judged, like the angel at the final harvest.

Passion and Glorification. All the Gospels end with the majestic narratives of the passion and exaltation. In teaching this section, don't stop with the cross. Go beyond to the resurrection. If you say that we were saved by the cross of Jesus, how will you answer the students' questions about Easter Sunday? Do not tell them that the resurrection was a reward because Christ worked so hard, or that it is an apologetic proof of the divinity. This may be somewhat true, but it is not the principal reason for the resurrection. The resurrection was as essential to salvation as was the cross. "Christ died for our sins, and *rose again for our justification*" (Rom 4:25).

You must not view salvation only in terms of its tragedy and series of sad events. Salvation is a living event. All living events are in motion, in a fluid state. When you teach the redemption mystery, do so by presenting it as a journey through death to life and glorification, continuing in the sending of the Spirit and the establishing of the Church. Teach death, resurrection, ascension, the sending of Spirit and arrival of the Church as the broad arc of one continuous action. Redemption is not any one of these things, it is all of these actions. It is a movement, a passage, a passover.

So, do not be limited by cross-theology, and do not proclaim a dead Christ, for Jesus has risen from the dead and lives. We do not fix our eyes on the cross of Albercht Dürer — a contorted plague-Christ that caught the devotion of an earlier time. Our eyes are on the Christ of the resurrection — the Christ of the new Coventry cathedral, filling the altar with His glory. This is the Christ we proclaim, not an effeminate Christ who seems half dead. We announce not the pale horse, but the triumphant Rider on the white horse.

Therefore, when you teach Christ, do so within the outlines of the Gospel record, keeping the theme of salvation uppermost in your mind. Now, a word about the infancy narratives of Matthew and Luke. These are highly stylized and poetic stories about the birth of Jesus. They did not constitute the original kerygma but arose when the Christian community was maturing and was turning a contemplative gaze to the mystery of the incarnation. Read Fr. Carroll Stuhlmueller's pamphlet commentary on Luke in the *New Testament Reading Guide* (The Liturgical Press, Collegeville, Minn.) for a way of starting a lesson on this subject.

Make Christ Present

Always teach Jesus as one present. The temptation in dealing with an ancient record like a Gospel is to look at Christ as someone in the past. He is more than an ordinary historical figure; He lives now. Hence you must reveal Jesus as having a relevancy and urgency in the here and now. Take, for example, the Sermon on the Mount. Show your students the core sermon, which was a hot, polemic attack by Christ against the Pharisaic interpretation of the law. Then demonstrate how Matthew made additions from other sayings of Jesus to expand the original polemic into a broader program of Christian living, one that is addressed to the Church of today.

Compare the beatitudes of Matthew and Luke. Matthew has eight (nine, in the reckoning of some), and Luke has four. It is most probable that Luke has the original beati-

tudes, which were expanded by Matthew into eight. Matthew's
extra beatitudes are repetitions and additions, which as new
law were meant to correspond to the ten commandments of
the old law. The core beatitudes were meant to attack the
Pharisees and reassure the men of faith that the promises
of Isaiah 61 are now fulfilled in the arrival of the kingdom.
Today, however, these beatitudes of both Matthew and Luke
speak directly to the heart of the modern Christian.

When Jesus says, "Let your speech be yes, yes and no,
no" (Mt 5:37), tell your students that these words are di-
rected to them and not just to the Apostles. It is better to
state that Jesus *says* rather than Jesus *said.* Speak the Gospel
record as a living message that is both of the first and the
twentieth centuries. From the Gospel comes the sword that
pierces the conscience of our generation.

Liturgy

The liturgy witnesses Christ as Mediator. We have been
plagued with so many mediators in recent Christian piety
that they have become like the household gods of the Romans
and have obscured the unique mediatorship of Jesus. We
do not need to eliminate intercessory prayers, but we must
restore Jesus as the one Mediator between God and man
Practically every oration in the liturgy begins with Deus —
"Oh Father!" And they end with the formula, "Through
Jesus Christ, our Lord." Pick the Epistle to the Hebrews and
read about Jesus standing in heaven before the Father, showing His wounds and making intercession for us. Hebrews describes the liturgy in heaven, which is imaged for us in the
Mass and the sacraments. Our earthly liturgy is a shadow of
the heavenly one where Jesus holds the central position as
Mediator.

Teach this to your students, for it focuses attention on
the proper sweep of the liturgy. We go toward the Father,
through Jesus.

The liturgical year unfolds the mystery of Jesus' life and

works. It arranges the revelation about Christ so that we can contemplate it in stages and celebrate it. As we grow older each year, our renewed contact with the mystery initiates us more deeply into its significance. Our yearly return to the events of Christ's life may seem repetitious to some, but it is as necessary as a cabinetmaker's rubbing of his wood to bring forth the beauty of the grain. The passing years bring wisdom, our contact with the eternal wisdom of our Lord makes us know more truly the meaning of salvation and the significance of the Christ event.

The liturgy of the sacraments reveals Jesus. Sacramental moments cause a Christ-encounter. In Penance, Marriage, and the other sacraments the Christian meets the Lord Jesus; if he doesn't then the sacrament has been a failure for him. Liturgy is not just a place to read about Christ; it is a place to meet Him. In the novel *Catcher in the Rye* Holden Caulfield sings, "If a body catch a body. . . ." His sister Phoebe rebukes him, "No, Holden. If a body meet a body. . . ." In other words there must be personal involvement.

Too often spiritual writers on the moral and ascetical life have unwittingly depersonalized and mechanized our approach to Christ, and tricked us into an illusion of spirituality that doesn't exist. This may be seen in their exhortations to the pure intention. Make the pure intention and everything will go well. Moral theologians are quoted about the virtual intention which hovers over the act. Yet somehow the uncanny feeling survives that this is not quite so. What I mean is that the intention is not enough. It is too cool, too cerebral. Unless there is personal engagement, the intention will seem to vanish. We need the habit of plunging into reality and not floating over it. If this habit is not acquired, how will we know what it means to encounter the person of Jesus in the sacraments.

Unless you practice this constantly, unless you are engaged in the very concreteness of things, "under the wings of God," you may really not meet Jesus in sacramental events. To go to

Mass and offer it up for a certain intention is not enough. You must move right in to the mystery of the celebration in order to meet Christ. Help your students meet their Savior in the sacraments.

Doctrine

Doctrine attempts to take the data of revelation about Jesus, synthesize it, and make it relevant for the Christian. Doctrine has dealt much with the moral Jesus, that is, the Jesus who is the model of holiness and the good life. Most meditation books center attention on Christ as the Exemplar of perfection. Jesus was kind to the widow of Naim and raised her son from the dead; Christians should be as compassionate as Christ. He did a good deed, we must perform good works. This is using Christ as a moral inspiration. But if this is all that your catechesis consists of, you might just as well use Albert Schweitzer or Tom Dooley. There have been very fine men in the world whom we uphold for admiration, but there is something very different about Jesus. Of course we must imitate the splendid deeds of Christ, but this is insufficient. He is not simply to be admired and imitated. There is more to Christ.

Doctrine also deals with the psychological Jesus. At the moment the studies on this subject are minimal and inadequate. Some hope that we are on the verge of a great, new Christological insight, but few know whether our generation will see it. Studies on the psychology of Jesus concern themselves with the reconciliation of His divine and human knowledge. They raise questions such as these: How could He reconcile in His own consciousness His awareness that He was God with the gradual growth of His awareness of human realities? How could He be learning and yet know everything? How could He be a real man and yet have the astonishing vision of God? How could these coexist in the same affectivity and consciousness? How could He be hurt, tired, angry? How could He have these fallible human emotions when He possesses that startling flash of the beatific vision to calm everything down? And then there are questions about His messianic consciousness. We do not have many answers to these questions. I feel we should leave this issue to the research theologians and give them time to think and ponder this great mystery of the inner life of Jesus.

The real challenge to the catechist is to teach the *onto-logical Jesus*. This is the necessary and perfect complement to the first step mentioned above, namely, the vision of Christ as our model. St. Paul uses the expression "in Christ Jesus" over 130 times. He tells soldiers, slaves, housewives, Jewish clergymen, and Christian bishops they must live "in Christ Jesus." He spoke less about imitating Jesus than about living *in* Him. I admit that this is the toughest idea for the catechist to get across, but its difficulty must be surmounted. I admit also that this is a mystery before which I falter, and yet one which I feel impelled to face.

Here are some thoughts that may help. While Jesus was on earth, He had a particular consciousness and affectivity. He was aware of His surroundings and had certain feelings toward them. Term these the two poles of His existence. On the other hand we have our students of today with their own awareness of life and special reactions to the things that happen to them. Somehow the students must undergo a transformation. Their own awareness and affectivity must change so that it is the same as Christ's. Some kind of identity between the consciousness and affectivity of Christ and that of the students must be established.

How is this done? Primarily it occurs through acts of faith and the sacraments which are the normal complement of faith. By an act of faith I do not mean the recital of a formula, but rather a personal submission to Jesus as Savior. Take the example of Christ and the woman of Samaria. Christ comes to Jacob's well. He is tired. It is the middle of the day. He rests by the well and wants a drink of water to satisfy His thirst. A woman comes to get water. Jesus becomes aware of the woman, develops a feeling toward her and makes a decision to change her life. It is possible for us through serious and attentive thinking to analyze Christ's inner reaction to this event.

The well of Jacob story happened two thousand years ago. Has the inward attitude which Jesus possessed at that moment evaporated? No, it still exists. Here is an analogy. Every man carries at a given moment the full burden of his past. He is everything he was. That is why psychologists dredge up the past life of disturbed patients, and show them it is not so past at all. It is in fact quite present. An adult who acts like a child at times betrays a fixation born twenty years before and surviving now to embarrass and torment the person. Men carry with them the baggage of their past, bearing in themselves the whole complexus of awarenesses and emotional outbursts of their previous years.

When it comes to Jesus, not only do all the interior attitudes of His life survive, because He is human as we are, but these survive in a special way because He is God. Each of the moments of His historical existence had a transforming power that transcends its action in a particular historic space and time, and works again in successive ages of history. The interior meaning of the well of Jacob story is carried forward in history and becomes active whenever a Christian contacts it in faith, whenever a liturgical assembly celebrates it. Then Jesus, who is everything He was, acts again on whoever surrenders to Him. Jesus brings the transforming power of His own attitude to bear upon the Christian who wishes to be transformed by Him. If His attitude was one of compassion and conversion for a sinful creature, then He can produce this attitude in us by the mysterious power of His Holy Spirit.

Jesus, then, does not only exist outside you as a model to be admired. He is One who *groans* through His Spirit in your soul to transform you. The moral Jesus is too extrinsic a catechesis. You must link it to a catechesis of the Pauline "in Christ Jesus" if you want to be a success in teaching this central mystery of our religion: Jesus our Savior.

Dogmatic theologians take their starting point from an existential, personal, and dynamic view of Jesus. Christ revealed Himself by acts in our own sphere of existence. John said: "We speak of what we have heard and seen, of what our hands have touched" (1 Jn 1:1). We must first see Jesus in His situation before formulating a doctrinal statement about Him. To study Him apart from His existence is unrealistic. The Gospel signs of His existence are continued by the signs of His life in the contemporary Church. Show this unity of Jesus, "yesterday, today, and forever."

Christ's actions are not merely human, but are an effective invitation to a new life. Study His conversion of Nathanael, the Samaritan woman, and Magdalen. Jesus never demands the impossible, but neither does He side with our sins. The encounter with Christ demands reaction, change, and conversion. His catechesis is always progressive. The dynamic view of Jesus shows Him as leading men to deeper faith by means of a fuller revelation of Himself. Catechists must present a Jesus who will change the lives of those who hear about Him.

The catechesis of Jesus must be *personal*. Doctrine does not intend to black the personal vision of the Lord. Hold up Christ as one who says "I to Thou." Teach Him as one truly interested in the people of His generation. To do this well you must ask yourself the question, "Who is the Christ of our times?" I asked Gustave Weigel, S.J., this question one time and he replied, "The Christ of the nameless man, the lonely and alienated man puzzled and frightened by the oceans of men and conflicting thoughts and cosmic forces that threaten his utter ruin." Whether you agree or not, still some answer must be found so that the person of Jesus addresses the real person of our age.

Witness

Pierre Charles says in his meditations: "How can I see Christ, if I do not see Him in Christians?" You are the only possibility for the parousia of Christ in this world. If you did not exist the world could not see Jesus. Many today say that Pope John was a *glimpse* of Jesus. You may talk much about Christ, but if you do not live your message, then you are not a true catechist. The members of the Christian community teach Jesus by the interpretation given in the texture of their lives. The basic role of the Church is to be a witness, to be the light of nations.

A light is a light, precisely because it shines in a darkness. A candle doesn't shine very brightly when sunlight and electricity cancel it out. St. John says that the world is darkness and Christians are its light. The lives of the great saints are lights that announced the Lord Jesus. Christian artists witness Jesus in color and stone and poetry. Charismatic people introduce us in a striking way to the mystery of Jesus. The catechesis of Jesus, our Savior, reaches a climax when the catechist has a transparency that reflects Jesus alone.

An Appendix

The Cathedral Plan. The architecture of a church is a useful analogy for the catechesis of Jesus.

1. At the Door. Jesus announces the truths of faith, the deeds of salvation that call for conversion and faith. He baptizes those who surrender in faith. The door of the Church is the gate of heaven. The famed doorways of the medieval cathedrals illustrate this idea, showing Christ the King surrounded by the whole court of heaven, and inviting the world into the banquet hall of salvation.

2. In the Nave. Jesus leads us into the Church. Along the walls are the frescoes of the history of salvation that lead to the founding of the Church. The windows, too, speak of the events of revelation in both Testaments. All

leads to the founding of the Church, in which the risen
Christ dwells to confer His Holy Spirit to save men. In
other words it is only in the light of Christ that all sacred
history derives meaning. Noah and the flood will be little
more than a purified Babylonian myth unless linked to Christ
and the sacraments.

3. Sanctuary. In the liturgical event we encounter the living Christ. The Supper of the Lord proclaims His death and
resurrection. His love pours out to us in the gift of His
Spirit that we may bring it to the world. The priest-herald
announces the gospel, the good news, addressing the Christian assembly with the joy and urgency of the saving message, bringing history into mystery. He presents the gospel
signs as a present, central address to this community of faith,
which remembers Jesus and affirms that He is the Lord.

4. The Apse. Behold the *Kyrios* in glory. The Supper of
the Lord will be celebrated between His first coming in
great humility until His next coming in great glory. Gathered
before Him is the *community of the end of days*, waiting
in hope for the glory. It knows it will not be overwhelmed
by the powers of darkness, whose appearance is one of the
"woes" of the end-time. Here is the "little flock" to whom
God will give His reign (Lk 12:32).

As an image, then, the holy space of worship is its own
witness to the meaning of Jesus, who is the Center and
Power of all catechesis.

Chapter 4 ✝ The Holy Spirit

Not since the age of the Fathers has there been so much renewed interest in the Holy Spirit. For centuries he has been the forgotten Person of the Trinity, but Pope Paul in his address at the formal opening of the third session of the Second Vatican Council had much to say about the presence and working of the Holy Spirit in this age. I will devote the major part of this chapter to the recital of the New Testament testimonies about the Spirit, as the basis for a renewed catechesis of the Spirit.

Gabriel told Mary that she would be overshadowed by the power of the Most High, and sanctified so that she could receive Him by whom all things were made. This overshadowing is an image that is heir to the Old Testament manifestation of God in the cloud (*Shekinah*) and in the glory (*Kabod*). The cloud was His visible presence and the glory was the radiant outpouring of His light, a light so brilliant that it was blinding. The face of Moses shone with this light and had to be veiled because the people could not bear to look at him. This cloud and glory overshadowed Sinai at the great covenant scene of the ten commandments, and rested upon the cherubim of the ark during the tent days of the tribal confederacy. It overshadowed the inner sanctuary of the temple during the dedication ceremonies by Solomon.

Ezekiel saw this overshadowing glory depart from the temple but predicted that it would return. In the magnificent poem in Isaiah 60 the return of the glory is foretold: "Arise, shine, for your light has come, and the glory of the Lord has risen upon you" (Is 60:1). This cloud of glory which

41

led Israel to salvation from Egypt across the sea to the promised land was the visible, dynamic presence of God in the world. When the Bible speaks about the Holy Spirit it means the presence of God's dynamic action in the Church and the world.

The Spirit-glory which departed from the temple in the vision of Ezekiel now returns and overshadows the Virgin Mary and accomplishes the incarnation of Jesus.

At the visitation the Spirit comes again and fills Elizabeth with the knowledge that Mary will have a child and that this child is the Lord. "Why is this granted to me that the mother of my Lord should come to me?" (Lk 1:43.) Filled with this same Spirit, her husband Zachary sings the *Benedictus*, which is a hymn about his son, who will be a prophet and will prepare the way of the Lord. The Spirit descends upon Simeon that he may know Jesus, for the old man had been promised he would not see death until he had seen the Lord Christ. The prophetic circles of ancient Israel often went into an ecstasy of dance and song when the spirit took hold of them. Now again the Spirit descends to bring people to the joy of music and poetry to express their feeling about the good news.

John the Baptist is filled with the Spirit in the womb of his mother. His first message on Jordan's bank is that one is coming who will baptize in Spirit and fire. The fire image is often associated in Scripture with the Spirit. It was a pillar of fire as well as a pillar of cloud which led Israel in the desert. A cloud and fire enveloped Sinai at the covenant. Jesus would preach that He came to set fire upon the earth and send His spirit into the hearts of men. Pentecost is a gift of the Spirit in the form of fiery tongues. The parallel of fire and Spirit is a typical poetic device of the Hebrews.

In Malachi 3:1–5, the Messiah is described as one who came to cleanse the temple and purify the sons of Levi as a man uses fire to take the impurities out of gold. Fire is an image of purification and transformation. The Holy Spirit will accomplish actually what the metaphor of fire suggests.

The Holy Spirit comes down on Jesus at the Jordan baptism so that the dignity of Him who is baptized may not be hidden. "He on whom you see the Spirit descend and remain, this is he who baptizes with the Holy Spirit" (Jn 1:33). The servant poem of Isaiah (42:1–4) says that the sign of the messianic servant will be the one on whom the Father sends the Spirit.

Jesus often talked about the Spirit. In His conversation with Nicodemus under the night sky, He spoke about a rebirth in water and the Spirit. And as the conversation proceeded, the water image drops out and only the Spirit is talked about. He contrasts the life of the flesh (sarx) with the life of the Spirit which He brings. The flesh is the unredeemed man, the life of the Spirit is the existence of man saved by Jesus and introduced into the higher realm of God.

The same is true of Christ's conversion talk at the spring of Jacob with the Samaritan woman. When she is feeling uncomfortable because He has accused her of harlotry, she shifts the conversation to problems of liturgy. Christ tells her not to worry about cultic rivalries for the day is coming when real worship will be in Spirit and truth. It is at this point that St. John makes the first of the three affirmations about God, namely, "God is Spirit" (Jn 4:24). Later on he will say that God is Love and that God is Light.

In another place Jesus speaks of blasphemy against the Spirit in contrast to blasphemy against the Son of Man. "And everyone who speaks a word against the Son of Man will be forgiven; but he who blasphemes against the Holy Spirit will not be forgiven" (Lk 12:10). By blaspheming against the Holy Spirit He means rejecting the inbreaking of the kingdom of God, and dismissing the clearly evident signs of its arrival. It is pardonable not to see the humiliation of the suffering servant and royal son of God, but to reject the demonstration of the reign of God in the power of the Spirit, as it is experienced in the life of the Church, is outside the sphere of forgiveness altogether. St. Peter is eminently one who blasphemes against the Son of Man (denial scene: cf. Mk 14:66–72). He is forgiven (cf. Mk 16:7) and thereafter obeys the Holy Spirit.

Before His departure from this earth Jesus promised us another Consoler to abide with us, the Holy Spirit who would teach us the meaning of the works of the Lord and lead us to witness Him before the world. "The Holy Spirit whom the Father will send in my name, will teach you all things, and bring to your remembrance all that I have said to you" (Jn 14:26).

Pentecost: John and Luke

New Testament writers agree that the giving of the Spirit was withheld until after the resurrection and exaltation of Jesus. They do not agree about the manner and time of the coming of the Spirit. Only John and Luke tell the story, and their accounts differ in every way except that the events took place at Jerusalem. John says the ascension took place between the appearance to Mary on Easter morning and His manifestation to the Apostles that evening. On that evening Christ bestowed the fellowship of the Spirit on them. It was the second great divine breathing on man, the first being at Genesis, later stifled by man's sin, the second here in John's account and witness to the fulfillment of the promise. St. Paul seems to agree with this account. He does not distinguish much between the resurrection and ascension as separate events. He describes the vision of Jesus on the Damascus road as the same which Peter and the other disciples saw, the postascended Christ (cf. 1 Cor 15:5–7).

Luke gives a different idea of Pentecost, shaping his account by an elaborate typological and theological scheme. He emphasizes the waiting period between the resurrection and ascension (cf. Lk 24:49; Acts 1:3). He treats the ascension and resurrection as separate events and then waits ten more days for the Spirit. Our liturgy follows the scheme of Luke. He used existing rabbinic Passover-Pentecost liturgy as the model for describing the new Pentecost. Passover was the memory of the exodus deliverance and Pentecost was a festival of the ten commandments, the sealing of the covenant at Sinai. The descent of the Holy Spirit becomes the sealing of the redemptive work of Jesus accomplished at the Christian Passover. The pentecostal law of Sinai finds perfect completion in the pentecostal fires of the Spirit.

The Lukan Pentecost is rich in teaching about the Spirit. St. Peter tells the crowd that this event was foretold by Joel the prophet who claimed that on the messianic day of the Lord the Spirit of God would pour out upon the earth. Now under the impulse of the Spirit, sons and daughters shall prophesy, i.e., bear vital witness of Jesus to the world. The Spirit will cause young men to have visions and old men to have dreams. The visions do not refer to apparitions in mysterious grottos but rather to the keen insight given by the Spirit to help the Christian "see" into the true meaning of things from God's viewpoint. The dreams of old men are the same things as the visions of the young, being set up in the text of Joel according to the Hebrew poetic parallel in which the second statement reaffirms the first.

These words in a special way are addressed to catechists. When the Spirit comes you are going to see. What our Church needs today is not people who can chatter answers to catechism questions but people who can understand the world in which they live, people who can interpret reality. Your role as a teacher is to take the diverse experiences of the student and make sense out of them. Your role as a catechist is to take the diverse existences and experiences of your students and give them a Christian interpretation. How can you do this if you do not advert to their experiences, and if you do not attend to the interior testimony of the Spirit who comes to give you the necessary vision?

Do you believe you have received the Holy Spirit? Do you think He has something to do with your Christian life? What happened at Baptism and Confirmation? What happens when you sing of Him, "Gift of God most high"? Do you realize it must mean something for your classroom work that you shall prophesy and have visions and dreams? You need this understanding to interpret the meaning of your students' lives. That is what they want from you. They do not want clever, pious sayings. They want to know what life is all about, and what Christianity has to say about it.

You have the outpouring of the Spirit to help you. The Apostles went with Jesus for three years, and somehow seemed weak. They didn't even show up for the crucifixion. They were huddled in fear and cowardice on the day of the resurrection. They had three years of catechism class with the best Teacher who ever lived. And look what happened. But what did Jesus say? He said: "You need something else. You need the Holy Spirit. Wait here until He comes, and then you will know what I meant when I told you these things."

The Holy Spirit gives insight into the meaning of Scripture and into the meaning of life. "On my menservants and my maidservants in those days, I will pour out my Spirit; and they shall prophesy. And I will show wonders in the heavens above and signs on the earth beneath, blood, fire and vapor of smoke; the sun shall be turned into darkness and the moon into blood, before the day of the Lord comes. And it shall be that whoever calls on the name of the Lord shall be saved" (Acts 2:18–21). This is apocalyptic poetry, a typical Semitic way of describing a crisis, using cosmic catastrophes to symbolize the upheaval of the human order. It is not necessary to scan the skies for bloody moons or black suns. The real meaning is that the arrival of the Spirit marks a crisis in human history in which men are challenged to accept a new order, a new creation, a new covenant, a new Church.

Our Church today, like the one of Pentecost square, is an outpouring of the Spirit. This is what gives our Church its fluidity and dynamism, its resistance to rigidity, its ability to adapt to a new culture in every new generation. It is because the Church is the outpouring of the Spirit and not the decree of a law. This is why Paul told the Church it must not seek salvation under the law, for Christians are above the law, but rather seek redemption in the love of Jesus. This does not mean we cannot have laws and organizational procedures. But do not think that cleverly contrived organizational procedures are the Church. When the present organizational mold does not fit, the Church must shed it and seek a new one.

Under the impulse of the Spirit, the Church must be on the move. The Church is the river of God that gladdens the city of man. We cannot be a river unless we are allowed to flow. The river that does not flow falls back on itself and becomes stagnant. But the Church must be the wellspring which Jesus described to the Samaritan woman, flowing outward for eternal life.

The Church's first experience of the Holy Spirit in the days following Pentecost was phenomenal. He worked so mightily "that the company of those who believed were of one heart and soul" (Acts 4:32). How is the unity of the Church produced? Is it produced by law, by rules, by the nagging of superiors or preachers? The only way in which genuine love can melt and mold the people of God into unity is through the presence and mighty work of the Spirit. Catechists must implore the Spirit to come and make this unity.

It is time once again to think of our Church charismatically. In such a Church each member sees his role as a gift or charism of the Spirit. Hence nurses, teachers, janitors, gas-station attendants, salesmen, and executives all view their role in the world as resulting from an impulse of the Spirit. I know of a nurse who deliberately takes night work so that she will have time to stop by each bed and say a prayer for the patient. This nurse sees her role as Christian savior as well as the naturally compassionate woman who cares for the ill. The Vatican Council has leaned to using the charismatic structure suggested by Paul in his first letter to Corinth, Chapters 12 and 13.

"There are varieties of gifts but the same Spirit. . . . To each is given the manifestation of the Spirit for the common good. To one is given the utterance of wisdom, to another the utterance of knowledge, to another faith, to another the working of miracles, to another prophecy" (1 Cor 12:4–11). After Paul enumerates the diverse ministries to which the Spirit can impel the Christian, he writes that the greatest ministry of all is love. The supreme gift of the Spirit is charity which makes brilliance and martyrdom and concern for the poor assume real value. Read his hymn to love in Chapter 13.

Testimony. Another idea about the Spirit which the New Testament stresses is the testimony of the Spirit. There are two ways in which He can bear testimony, externally and internally. The external mediation of the Spirit comes infallibly from the Church in her evangelical posture and sacramental action. This mediation is infallible, though still dependent on the receptivity of the student. Christians can receive the Holy Spirit through the solemn proclamation of the word of God, the sacraments and genuine Christian love.

There is also an interior testimony. When you are reading a passage of the Bible in a quiet and prayerful attitude, you will often gain an insight that relates the passage in a special way to your personal life. Somehow you become identified with the passage, not so much in an intellectual way, as a scholar who suddenly solves a textual problem, but in a personal manner that moves you to deeper charity. This testimony also occurs when some great religious truth achieves a transparency for you that did not previously exist. You are often told that when Christians gather in the name of Jesus, He is there in the midst. One day you come to such a gathering and you truly realize that it is so. The Spirit's interior testimony has given you an experience of this old truth.

I am not referring here to some extraordinary ecstatic event or a "Jesus-jumpin'" phenomenon described in novels about the pentecostal religions. I simply mean the normal contemplative insight that any sincere Christian can experience who is prayerfully attentive to the interior testimony of the Spirit given to us in the sacraments. St. Paul knew there could be a problem in this so he says that one gift of the Spirit is the discernment of spirits (1 Cor 12:10) to separate the true from the false. The spirit of discernment resides in the Church to help you from declaring anything which is contrary to the brethren. Each Christian will always have a responsibility to the brethren who are the Church that helps determine the authentic testimony of the Spirit.

The Spirit Is the Holy Spirit of Truth. God knows we are looking for truth in the Church. Biblically, truth is not so much something to be taught as something to be done. It is not a matter of belief so much as action. That was one of the troubles with our former catechesis, which emphasized truth only as something to know. I realize that there was also an emphasis on action, but its immediacy was not so evident. In the biblical sense something becomes true mainly when it is done. That is why St. Paul insisted that we do the truth in love. This is why we have the Holy Spirit, in order that He may move us to do the truth. This is the meaning of the Spirit of truth.

The Spirit unlocks the mystery of the Bible. I have seen so many catechists discouraged at the thought of using the Bible in catechesis. "How will I be able to do it?" Yet you have been given the Spirit to help you. It is the letter that kills but it is the Spirit which quickens the holy page to life. This does not absolve you from studying the Bible and the many aids which abound today, but it keeps alive the basic idea that the Spirit breathes within the lines of Scripture and waits for the faithful submission to His action there.

It is the Spirit who imprints the character on the Christian when he receives the sacraments of baptism, confirmation, and holy orders. Do not teach the character passively as a sort of static stamp. The character is the brand of Jesus put into the Christian by the Spirit to help the Christian identify with the attitudes of Christ. This character is constantly at work; it is not passive. It is by means of the Spirit-branded character that we can be in motion toward the Father. I will explain this further when we cover the subject of baptism.

In the Acts the Spirit descended upon the seven deacons and filled them with wisdom. Stephen, full of the Spirit and faith, wrought wonders among the people. His adversaries were not able to resist the wisdom and Spirit by which he spoke. In the courtroom he was radiant with angelic brightness, and all who looked on him thought they saw the face of an angel. His wise defense confuted the court of stiff-necked men, uncircumcised in heart and ears and resisting the Holy Spirit. Stephen beheld the heavens opened and full of the Spirit was able to see the glory.

The deacon Phillip by the power of the Spirit was able to drive out unclean spirits, and convert the official of the palace of Candace, queen of Ethiopia. Ananias was sent to Paul after the Damascus event in order that the blinded convert might regain his sight and be filled with the Spirit. The Spirit's mighty action changed Paul's blindness into Christian light and made him a vessel of election worthy to bear the name of the Lord.

Led by the Spirit, Peter healed Aeneas the paralytic at Lydda, and raised Tabitha, the woman of good works, to life at Haifa. It was the Spirit who gave Peter the rooftop vision of food. Armed with this vision he went to convert the house of Cornelius. "While Peter was still speaking, the Holy Spirit fell on all who heard the word. And the believers from among the circumcised who came with Peter were amazed for the gift of the Holy Spirit had been poured out even on the Gentiles" (Acts 10:44).

Think of what marvelous deeds Paul did in the name of Jesus and under the power of the Spirit. At Cyprus he vanquished Elymas the sorcerer; and healed the cripple of Lystra, and baptized his own jailer after an earthquake. At Ephesus he brought the people to speak with the gift of tongues and prophecy. There, even handkerchiefs touched to his body healed diseases and terrified evil spirits. "And a number of those who practiced magic arts brought their books together, and burned them in the sight of all; and they counted the value of them and it came to fifty thousand pieces of silver. So the word of the Lord prevailed and grew mightily" (Acts 19:19–20). At Troas, by the Spirit, Paul raised to life a man who fell asleep during his sermon, and who had fallen out of the window and was killed. At Miletus Paul said, "The Holy Spirit testifies to me in every city that imprisonment and affliction await me" (Acts 20:23). At Caesarea, before Felix, Festus, and King Agrippa, the power of the Spirit was so great that Agrippa was moved to say, "In a short time you think to make me a Christian" (Acts 26:28). On the island of Melita the Spirit protected Paul from a poisonous serpent. And it was the Spirit who brought Paul to Rome as the herald of Jesus.

Paul's teaching about the Spirit in the epistles is well worth noting. "My speech and my message were not in the plausible words of wisdom, but in the demonstration of Spirit and power" (1 Cor 2:4). Your classroom catechesis must be in the manner of Paul. As he did not put first strength into the manipulation of human wisdom, neither should you. His catechesis was a demonstration of Spirit and power. You can learn this basic lesson from Paul that your prophetic vocation implies that you are a mediator of the Holy Spirit above all. Lesson plans and visual aids and clever techniques do not replace the fundamental vocation to show forth the Spirit.

"He that raised Jesus from the dead will give life to your mortal bodies also through the Spirit who dwells in you" (Rom 8:11). Paul speaks to the soldiers of Christ: "Take the helmet of salvation, and the sword of the Spirit which is the word of God. Pray at all times in the Spirit, with all prayer and supplication" (Eph 6:17–18). In these days you must experience new life from the Spirit to quicken your mortal and easily discourageable frame. You must have the aggressiveness of soldiers and the prayerfulness of contemplatives. Paul calls Christian heralds to pray much. Your catechesis stems from contact with the Spirit who is readily met on the ground of prayer.

Liturgy

The pentecostal hymns stress the dynamism of the Spirit. He is the outgoing power of God present in the Church. In the baptismal ceremony the candidate is sealed with the Spirit. This seal puts the mark or character of the Lord Jesus on the Christian. The Spirit-sealed Christian can now properly worship God in Spirit and in truth. Such a Christian acquires the attitudes of Christ, especially His attitude toward our Father. It is the Spirit who helps us be dedicated to the death-life paradox of the redemptive mystery of Christ.

When the word is proclaimed in liturgy, it is the presence of the Spirit bearing testimony which makes possible our understanding of the truth. Such an understanding is not simply a passive comprehension, but a doing of the truth in love.

Liturgical events mark the official presence of God. The fresh breath of the Spirit gives a new awareness of this presence. He truly renews the face of the earth. His pentecostal fire makes every liturgical assembly an upper room. At all great sacramental moments, the Spirit moves over the waters.

The Spirit is the activist of the liturgy bringing alive the biblical words to make them create the assembly anew. He works in the sacramental actions to fulfill their destinies. Liturgical events move under the press of the Spirit whose urgency is demanded by the nature of this action. There is an infallibility about liturgy which operates when the Spirit finds an attitude of openness and receptivity in the congregation. The Spirit's chief milieu is the freedom of the winds, as Jesus said to Nicodemus. The Spirit must find such relaxed freedom too in the Christians who come to worship. Then He makes men of the field of bones. To conclude this chapter I offer you some biblically rooted questions on the Spirit, which you may use in a class or in a discussion club. As a preparation read Guardini's *The Lord*, pages 435–438. To introduce the discussion read John 16:5–14:

1. How close were the Apostles to Jesus during His earthly life?
2. As a rabbi, how would He have trained His Apostles?
3. Did the Apostles question Jesus, observe His deeds?
4. How did they react to the impressiveness of His gestures?
5. How deep was their understanding of Jesus?
6. How closely did they identify themselves with His intentions?
7. Was their failure to understand Him due to the greatness of His message and the short time available to grasp it?
8. Didn't they gradually come to know Him through personal discussion and progressive adjustment of their lives?
9. Was their lack of comprehension due to the difficulty of Christ's teaching?
10. Was it due to their inability to relate properly to Jesus — to have faith in Him?
11. To say that they did not believe, does this mean they were not sympathetic and generous?
12. Basically what is missing in their relation to Jesus?
13. Why must you take care not to blur the meaning of faith here?
14. What happened after the pentecostal experience in the upper room?
15. What made Peter pass from the questioning, puzzled fisherman to a proclaiming, believing bishop?
16. Did Peter change because of a newly acquired self-control?

17. How does recognition generally come? (Who understands nature best: the scientist or the man who lives in nature? Who understands music best but the man who lives in music? Who understands Jesus best but the man who lives in Jesus?)

18. Where does Christ come from? What does He live from? From what power does He draw His strength?

19. As a real Christian, where did you come from? What do you live from? Where do you derive your strength?

20. What does the spiritual man mean in St. Paul?

21. What does it mean to say that the spiritual man is a mystery?

22. Can the world understand the spiritual man?

23. Does being a mystery man mean you are wiser, stronger, and more talented than others?

24. Can we say that the relation of the unbeliever to the Christian is analogous to the relation of the Apostles to Jesus before Pentecost?

> "Grieve not the Holy Spirit, by whom you
> were sealed unto the day of redemption."
> (Eph 4:30.)

Chapter 5 ❧ The Church

Not too many years ago I felt like Diogenes who carried a lantern and peered into people's faces, with the persistent question on his lips, "Where can I find an honest man?" I was looking for an honest and more complete answer to the question, "What is the Church?" Today this query is universally asked, and by an assembly no less august than the Vatican Council. Although Pope Pius XII's encyclical on the *Mystical Body* did much to deepen our realization of the Church as a living organism, as the living Christ, there have always been pedagogic difficulties in presenting the mystery that is the Church under this image. In recent years, and preeminently in the conciliar debates over the Church and in the Vatican Council's *Constitution on the Church*, attention has been focused on the notion of the Church as the people of God. Some reflections on this theme ought, therefore, to be of some value in penetrating more deeply the meaning of the Church.

The New Testament reinterprets the theology of the Old. The Christian community of Jews and Gentiles is the new people of God. In the Septuagint the Greek word *laos*, "people," applies to those of the same race and language. It is used fifteen hundred times, but it has the additional technical meaning of describing Israel as the chosen nation (cf. Heb 11:25). The New Testament adopts this term for the Christian community.

The Old Testament highlights God's purpose for Israel in this world. Genesis describes, under the prophetic interpretation, God's selectivity. As the nations appear on earth, God directs His attention to Seth, Noah, and then to Abraham.

It is especially with Abraham that the idea of the people of God is born. God encounters this patriarch on the plains of Haran and makes a proposition. "Go from your country and your kindred and your father's house to the land that I will show you. And I will make of you a great nation, and I will bless you, and make your name great so that it will be a blessing" (Gn 12:1–2). A Semitic blessing was the transmission of power or life, usually by means of a physical gesture, as the placing of one's hand on the other, as when Isaac put his hand on Jacob and in turn the son placed his hand on Isaac's thigh that from the loins of his father he might obtain the procreative strength to carry on the family.

Now God blesses Abraham, assuring him that from him shall come a family and eventually at nation in which all other nations shall be blessed. The nation that would be a source of blessing and light to the others is Israel, a nation-church. Abraham agreed to submit to God's plan, had a harrowing experience at Mount Moriah, but lived to see his family survive and take its place in history.

As the years roll by, they multiply greatly and migrate to Egypt during the time of the great famine when their country-man, Joseph, is the second most powerful man of the realm. After a few centuries the Egyptians look with suspicion and distaste at the Semitic enclave to the north and decide to make slaves of them. Now the God of the patriarchs appears to Moses and plans the freedom movement. God wants to transform the Hebrews from a slave caste into His own people who are to serve a divine purpose before the world.

God enters into a debate through His representative Moses with the Pharaoh. He sends the plagues as signs of judgment upon this nation that wishes to frustrate His will. Then follow the marvels of salvation — the victory at the Reed Sea, the streams of the desert, bread and meat from heaven. All these miracles of grace reach a climax at Sinai where God forms His Church, His assembly. They key text to understanding the Sinai event is Exodus 19:3–6.

"And Moses went up to God, and the Lord called to him out of the mountain saying, 'Thus shall you say to the house of Jacob, and tell the people of Israel: You have seen what I did to the Egyptians, and how I bore you on eagle's wings, and brought you to myself. Now, therefore, if you will obey my voice and keep my covenant, you shall be my own possession among all peoples; for all the earth is mine, and you shall be to me a kingdom of priests and a holy nation. These are the words which you shall speak to the children of Israel.'"

Real religion begins from above, not below. It is in God that initiative lies. That is why the emphasis is on what God has done for these people, lifting them up on eagle's wings and saving them from the tyranny of Egypt. If they agree to accept all the wonderful things God has done for them, He will make them into His people, and will fashion them into a priestly nation. Why a priestly nation? A priest is one who stands between God's throne of mercy and the cry of sinful man. However, do not restrict the idea of priest to the sacrificial minister of the altar. As God indicates in the above text, the very nation itself can function as a priestly medium. The vocation of Israel was to bring, from God's throne of mercy, light and salvation for a fallen world. They did accept this call with joy during the desert experience, albeit with some disappointing relapses. But as the years flowed on, Israel forgot her priestly vocation and soon ceased to think of her role as the light of nations.

This is best seen in the story of the prophet Jonah. God tells this Jewish prophet to go and preach repentance in Niniveh so that the pagans will not be destroyed by divine wrath. Jonah did not want to do this, so he took a boat for a city far away from Niniveh. God causes a storm to rise, while Jonah contentedly naps in the stateroom below. Up on deck the frightened sailors are praying for deliverance, while the prophet of God's people sleeps away. They get him and bring him to the deck. He tells them that the storm is his

fault because God is angry with him. They throw him into
the sea, and he is swallowed up into the darkness of death,
for to find redemption and resurrection, there must first be
a crisis and a death. This is why Jesus quoted this story in
the Gospel. After three days, Jonah is brought up from the
darkness and sent to preach to the Ninivites.

Jonah goes through the streets preaching, and finds everyone remarkably receptive. But he refuses to believe that God
will truly have mercy on the city. He climbs a hill overlooking the metropolis, folds his arms grumpily and awaits
the downfall of fire and brimstone. Since it was a hot day,
God caused a gourd to grow and spread out its leaves to
shade the distressed prophet. Then God made the tree wither
as quickly as He had created it. Jonah complained bitterly,
but God replied: "You pity the plant for which you did not
labor, nor did you make it grow. And should I not pity
Nineveh, that great city?" (Jon 4:10.) God reminds Jonah
that He is free to give mercy to whomever He wishes and
that Israel has not been faithful to its vocation to be the
light of nations.

Jeremiah reflected on this sad disavowal of Israel and
announced that she would no longer be the people of the
covenant, but God would create a new people. "Behold the
days are coming, says the Lord, when I will make a new
covenant with the house of Israel, not like the covenant
which I made with their fathers when I took them by the
hand to bring them out of the land of Egypt, my covenant
which they broke, though I was their husband. Now I will
put my law within them, and I will write it upon their hearts,
and I will be their God and they shall be my people" (Jer
31:31–34).

The old covenant had been written on tables of stone;
now it would be inscribed on the heart and become a deeply
personal relationship. In this most important of Jeremiah's
utterances the Old Testament reaches one of its peaks. Its
proper echo will be heard at the Last Supper when Jesus

confirms the blood of the new order. Since the light of the old people of God had gone out, He would have to light a new one.

St. Paul, in Chapter 9 of his letter to the Romans, meditates on a passage from Hosea (Hos 1:10; 2:23) and concludes that the prophetic vision has now been fulfilled, and that God has formed a new people. But the truly great text for seeing this fulfillment is Peter's first letter, 2:9 ff. He quotes the Exodus text mentioned above, and applies it to the Christian Church. God has commissioned the Christian community to be the light of nations which the old Israel had failed to become. Christ's Church is a royal priesthood, representing God's interests to all the nations, and the needs of the world to God. God establishes within this people, summoned from the darkness into the light of His brilliant self-disclosure, a missionary character — they are sent forth to be His emissaries.

"But you are a chosen race, a royal priesthood, a holy nation, God's own people, that you may declare the wonderful deeds of him who called you out of darkness into his marvelous light. Once you were no people, but now you are God's people; once you had not received mercy but now you have received mercy" (1 Pt 2:9 ff.).

The Church is the people of God in order to declare the works of Him who led them out of darkness. This is recitation theology, announcing God's mighty deeds to the world. When the joyous Apostles tumbled out of the Pentecost chamber they talked about the wonderful works of God.

In catechesis bring this view of the Church's vocation to your students. Do not let them think the Church is a safety valve for the emotions or a security symbol, nor let them repeat the grumpy mood of a Jonah who cannot see how God could bring salvation to others. The members of the Church are *called* for this declaration. The name of the old church was *Qahal Israel*. The Hebrew word *qahal* means "to call." Israel was a community, not by reason of the consent of the members, but rather because God had summoned them into existence. The new Church, too, is a called community. Hence the meaning of the wedding parable whose refrain is, "Come to the wedding!"

When Pope John wanted to call the council he experienced opposition, but his patience and good will surmounted this. His council opened on October 11, feast of the Motherhood of Mary. This feast recalled the Council of Ephesus when the Fathers hotly debated whether Mary was simply mother of the man Jesus or indeed the mother of God. They finally concluded that she was *theo-tokos*, mother of Jesus who was the son of God. The rejoicing crowds surged through the city bearing torchlights, cheering and singing praises to Mary the mother of God.

On the night before the Second Vatican Council opened, a quarter of a million people streamed into St. Peter's square. Like the Christians of Ephesus they held aloft thousands of lighted candles and cheered for John. He came to the balcony overlooking the crowd and said, "I hear you, I hear you, the people of God. Jesus hears you, and your council begins." John heard the authentic cry of the Spirit from God's people. In early December, after he had been sick for some time, he felt well enough to lead the *Angelus* from his window. At that time he said, "What a spectacle we see before us, the Church grouped before us. Behold its bishops, behold its priests, behold its Christian people. *A whole family here present, the family of Christ.*"

In summary, the term "people of God" is a technical phrase referring to the nation of Israel. The Bible shows that God intended to pick a nation to be a witness of His saving power in the world. Through a process of selection from Seth, Noah, through Abraham and Jacob, God's purpose narrowed to the choice of Israel. After a dramatic deliverance from Egypt when God became Yahweh — Lord of hosts and Savior — a covenant was sealed and the details of their mission in the world was settled. But God's people failed in their mission. The prophets lamented this rejection, and Jeremiah announced that God would covenant a new people. The New Testament claims that Jesus Christ, through His death and glorification, formed a new people. Paul agrees with this idea and confirms it in his meditation on Hosea. Peter uses the original Sinai charter text to support the existence of this new people, and the importance of their missionary posture in this world as light of nations, and a royal priesthood acting as unique mediator of God among men.

Liturgy

The best way for Christians to experience themselves as Church is in the act of worship. The visible gathering of the summoned assembly at the official presence of God is the ideal ground and moment of realizing the meaning of the Church. Our catechesis today must draw us away from the dark corners into the full light of the assembly. Liturgical renewal aims at washing away those elements which divide us from each other, and blind us from seeing our common unity. For too long Church gatherings have been like Ezekiel's field of dry bones. Today catechesis working with the liturgical renewal must help the Spirit to breathe mightily upon these bones and let them live again as Church. The Holy Thursday liturgy sings that God is love, and he who abides in love abides in God and God in him. The world says that love is God, but Christians affirm that God is love, for they know Him in their union with each other at the Eucharist.

Rightly performed and properly situated, the celebration of the Lord's Supper should bring the people of God to a heightened awareness of their unique existence and a sharpened appreciation of the inward bond which the risen Jesus forges among them. Hence the new architecture which locates the people close to the altar, the priest now in full view of the assembly because he faces them, and the participation decrees of the Vatican Council make it eminently more easy for this people to know themselves as community and, therefore, as Church. In this way the people of God most perfectly discover themselves as the praying community in movement toward God the Father, through Christ by the force of the Spirit.

In the light of these ideas catechists should see that a heavy-handed apologetic treatment of the Church now seems unsuitable. A defensive posture maintained for too long a time is uncreative and unproductive. Today the inner nature of the Church must be proclaimed. The fathers of the Vatican Council lead the way by speaking much of the Church as the people of God, the light of nations, and the servant of the poor. Catechists are not above their masters, and should, therefore, follow the example of their bishops.

This fresh emphasis on the Church as community will challenge catechists to search for fresh ways of initiating their students into this idea. It demands research into ways of providing genuine community experience for students, especially for teen-agers, emerging from their introspective period into social awakening. It will be hard to see the Church as community if the members never experience it as such, particularly in the liturgy. The Church of today is reassuming her posture as a dynamic, missionary community ready to enter into dialogue with the world, fearlessly facing the enormous problems of world hunger, atomic war, the revolution of rising expectations, the population explosion and birth control. Such is the new and exciting Church catechists can rightly present to the eager generation of our times.

Bible dialogue . . . People of God Our Father

Read: Exodus 19:3–6; Jonah; Jeremiah 31:31–34; Romans 9:24–26; 1 Peter 2:9 ff.

1. Is the phrase "people of God" a technical term in Scripture?
2. About how often does it appear?
3. What is the first clear idea the people have about God?
4. When did they come to know of Him as Creator?

5. What is the role of God's selective purpose for people?
6. Did Israel merit God's selection?
7. What element is the same in the Abraham and Sinai covenants?
8. What does Sinai text mean by "kingdom of priests"?
9. Are the levites to Israel what she is to the world?
10. Did Israel break the covenant?
11. How does Jeremiah consider Israel's breaking of the covenant?
12. How does the Jonah narrative illustrate Israel's breaking of the covenant?
13. How did Paul reflect on the idea of the people of God?
14. How does Peter answer the question about the meaning of the Church?
15. What is your feeling about this term "people of God"?
16. Could it make you a more dynamic Christian?
17. Does this idea aid our work in ecumenism?
18. In what way has our Church failed in her mission to be the light of nations and the city set on a hill?
19. Do you see the need to view the Church through the lens of many images, realizing there is a shortcoming in any single one (including people of God)?

Chapter 6 ✢ The Sacraments

Monsignor Martin Hellriegel often tells this story about one of his return trips to his native Germany. He was sipping coffee in a Bremen train station when a young Jewish fellow came up to sell him a newspaper. Noting that the man had a south German accent, the Monsignor asked him about his origin. The newsboy replied, "I am from Vienna, but I found my Lord Jesus Christ in Bremen." This statement rang in the Monsignor's mind all the way down to his hometown, moving him to visit his parish church before going home. There he knelt before the baptismal font and said, "Here I found my Lord Jesus Christ." It is a sacramental consciousness such as this which is a fond hope of modern catechesis.

Older catechism followed the scheme of creed — commandments — sacraments. Today the order is creed — sacraments — commandments. The older catechism's philosophy stemmed from questions such as "Where am I going, and how am I going to get there?" It was a goal-centered catechesis, seeing heaven as the end and all else as means to get there. The Apostle's Creed was taught as a summary of abstract statements about where we were going and why, and the commandments stood as the principal means of getting there. A great deal of energy poured out to illuminate the commandment-means, but left the sacraments out in the cold. Most teachers presented the sacraments also as means to heaven and obliquely, though unintentionally, indicated that they were not quite as powerful as the commandments. This was a pedagogical misfortune as well as theologically questionable.

Sacraments are not simply means to achieve salvation, they are the salvation event itself. The moment of baptism is an exact entry into salvation, so that the candidate can truthfully say, "I am saved." It is superstition to state that the sacraments are a sort of charm that have only functional significance, for sacraments are the mighty deeds of God wherein He saves His people.

The Apostles' Creed is the story of salvation and not a series of abstract propositions. It is the basis for evangelizing the student. Systematic theologians necessarily have erected abstract clarifications of the credal events, but evangelically the catechist must return to the event itself. In the creed we talk about events, not concepts. The sacraments are the way in which we enter into that salvation, and the commandments are signs of our commitment to the saving deed much more than they are means of achieving it. Keeping commandments is not salvation, for we are not under the law. Paul reminded the Romans that salvation is not reached through obedience to a law but through the power of Jesus Christ mediated to us through His sacraments. Salvation occurs first in the sacramental event; the commandments are signs of this salvation commitment and means to help us remain saved.

Bible

The Old Testament establishes the sacramental principle. When God touches time, and genuinely and visibly enters a given period of history, an exceptional divine-human encounter occurs. God only enters history for the purpose of saving man. One of his greatest historical interventions is described in the Book of Exodus. Here is the central theological moment of the Old Testament. The Exodus event is the kerygma of the old dispensation; it is the gospel of Israel, her primary salvation pattern. Do not confine the Exodus to the going-out from Egypt, rather include everything from the call of Moses at the burning bush, the plague narratives, the sea victory, the stations to Sinai, the covenant declaration on the mountain to the climactic ceremony of the covenant after the giving of the law. Exodus includes the pillar of fire and cloud, the bread and quail from heaven, the fountains that sprang up in the desert, and the formation of a churchly people with their moral and cultic imperatives.

Such are the broad perspectives of the Exodus. A scriptural view is rarely as antiseptically trim or mechanically restrained to one point as our Western mentalities would like. Biblical themes are fluid, in constant movement, repeated transpositionally.

The meaning of the Exodus is apparent. God is a Savior who liberates Israel from Egypt, forms this band of runaway slaves into a cultic community, known before the world as "His people." But what about the Israelites who lived many years after this epic event? How could they sincerely participate in the enthusiastic dance and hymn of Miriam, who took up the cymbal and led the people in a joyous shout to celebrate the victory over Egypt? How could subsequent Israelites experience that salvation event and show God their own sincere surrender to His obvious power? What was needed was an institution that could memorialize the event, capture the interior meaning of the event, make present its inner salvation power.

It was God's will that the paschal meal and the ceremony of the unleavened bread should be the institution whereby the event of the Exodus could survive in history. Event is preserved by institution. When future Israelites would gather at the paschal table, eat the unleavened bread, drink the new wine, and partake of the Passover lamb, they could truly experience the salvation power dynamically manifested in the Exodus, and demonstrate to God, as did their fathers before them, that they were ready to surrender to His saving work.

The psychology of an Israelite fluctuated between his memories and his expectations, and he tended to view his expectations in terms of his memories. The good Israelite at the paschal table not only recalled the past, but looked to the bright future in terms of the past. He looked for what he called the "day of the Lord." This much repeated expression of the Old Testament refers to the day when God will absolutely triumph over all His enemies. Christianity is the day of the Lord to which faithful Israel looked. The prophets often spoke of the days of the Lord, intermittent gleams of triumph and judgment, all of which foreshadowed the perfect great day. It is what Jesus meant when He said, "The kingdom of God is here!"

These Old Testament ideas of event and institution, memory and expectation are key thoughts for understanding the Christian sacraments. Jesus obviously wanted His sacramental system to function within the framework of the Exodus-Passover. Why does He deliberately celebrate the Passover meal just before He dies? Why does He intentionally arrive in Jerusalem precisely at Passover time, when the Exodus is commemorated? Why does He emphasize the unleavened bread and the paschal lamb? Why does He place His ceremony of new bread and new wine around the eating of the great lamb? Because He wants His Church to know that the Eucharist is an institution like the Passover, and that it memorializes the new salvation event about to take place.

It is Christ's will that sacraments should be seen against the framework of the Old Testament ideas of event and institution. Christ's own action from the upper room onward is an exodus, in which He marches from this life into the halls of death and then up to glory. As Luke 9:51 puts it: "When the days drew near for him to be lifted up, he set his face to go to Jerusalem." This lifting up refers both to His cross and to His glorification. Jesus is reproducing the march of the Israelites. His walking is a paschal walking; the journey from Galilee to Jerusalem is a solemn ritual procession in which Christ, corporately personalizing the people of God, strides forth to bring to its fullest meaning the archetypal passage of the Exodus pilgrims.

St. John's Gospel centers heavily on feasts and symbols.

It appears to be a series of liturgical homilies on the sacraments. Some suggest it is a result of John's Easter sermons to the newly baptized about the meaning of sacramental life. He has many journey scenes in his account. This seems to fit his sacramentary constantly within the Exodus framework. Here is a valuable pedagogical insight for catechists. Present catechesis emphasizes the static and impersonal approach to the sacraments. But the scriptural model describes saving events in terms of people on the march, a savior on the move. They are going from something worse to something better, through trial and fire into a land of promise. With the static approach can our students perceive sacraments in terms of movement from something worse to something better, a dynamic thrust from death to life? Sacramental catechesis has too often been a melange of wooden theological speculation, fashionable mysticism, and questionable impersonalism. It ought to partake of the sagalike modalities of the biblical page in which God, the Consuming Fire, melts His way into the consciousness of men and reshapes their lives. It is as personal as a conversation. Thus speaks the Lord of hosts! The placing of a wafer on our tongues should not be an embarrassing occurrence which would tie us up apologetically in the presence of a sophisticated Buddhist or latter-day humanist. It is a personal meeting with our Lord Jesus Christ which we joyously affirm in faith.

The miracles of Jesus are prototypes of the sacraments. Too often they are viewed exclusively in terms of divinity proofs or faith evokers. I would not deny that these elements are present, but the marvels of Jesus are parallel to the mighty acts of His Father in the Exodus, and both sets of deeds are continuing in the Church through the sacramental actions. In the cure of the paralytic who was lowered through the roof, the emphasis is on the salvation of the man, rather than the cure of his stiffened limbs. Almost by afterthought does Jesus turn and cure the man. This is a miracle of grace, of salvation from sin in which the cure serves as a sign for

the inner renewal of the man. Miracles are salvation acts in
which Christ presents signs of His kingdom of grace.

This does not mean that Christ has no compassion and
is not interested in the physical welfare of the blind and
diseased. He is as sad as anyone else in the face of human
misery, but philanthropy is not His primary concern, rather
it is salvation. The sacraments are the miracles of the Church
in the sense that they continue the mighty acts of Jesus in
the world today. He is again touching people with oil, bread,
wine, and the hand of mercy, bringing them from sin to grace.

The Fathers of the Church understood this view of the
sacraments. Father Jean Danielou has restored their insight
for our times in his two excellent works, *From Shadows to
Reality* and *The Bible and the Liturgy*. The miracles-sacra-
ments analogy is based on the principle of typology. God's
saving deeds in the Exodus were reinterpreted by the prophets
to describe the day of the Lord. These deeds found their
greatest realization in Jesus and continue now in the Church
and the sacraments. Hence the sacraments are the present
continuation of a heritage that began several thousand years
ago when God wrought His wonders in Egypt and the desert
of Sinai. This is why the liturgical texts for the sacraments
speak so much of the sacrifice of Abel, Abraham, and Melch-
isedech, of the lamb of God, of a water crossing, of the
marriage of Isaac and Rebekah — indeed of the whole story
found in revelation. The Bible is the event. Liturgy is the
institution.

Liturgy means incorporation into the most splendid of all
histories — that of salvation. It is the same God who acts
all the way through. The memory of the great biblical symbols is not a mere recollection, but a making present of God's
power as evidenced in the stories of revelation. In a sense,
liturgical action is itself a revelation insofar as each occurrence is an unveiling of God for the worshiper. Little by
little God discloses Himself in the cultic phenomenon so
that the Christian grows in knowledge and friendship with

his Lord. Keep in mind that the sacrament is an event, not a thing. It is a meeting ground for friends, holy because God is there, human because we are there.

The use of typology in sacramental theology is not just a clever matching of images nor a poetic pastime. To compare the resurrection of the widow's son by Elijah with the similar miracle wrought by Christ is not simply a test of scriptural gamesmanship. The analogy is real, not just an imaginative quirk. It is like the transposition of a theme in music in which the composer changes keys to establish a variety of moods. In scriptural transposition one image is laid upon the other, much as a painter uses layers of coloring to evoke depth. The transposition of biblical imagery illustrates the richness of salvation work. The analogy is interior, theological. Whenever analogies are being worked out both the image and the message must be kept in mind. Lining up the red ribbon of Rahab at the walls of Jericho with the ribbon of blood that flowed from the side of Christ is not only an essay in bad taste but a false and superficial, almost absurd application of the principle of typology. It is the sort of thing which revolts many from reading the more happy pages of the Fathers of the Church, because of these less felicitous usages.

Salvation events occurred in their own particular time and space. Men who live thousands of years later, and many thousands of miles from the original place raise the question, "How can I find God?" Men can find God in the same way He has always been reached, through historical moments in a particular space. It is through the sacraments that this can happen. But a mistake is sometimes made here. Mass catechesis frequently speaks of making Calvary present, as though the very rock and blood and lance somehow were here again. It is not the historical details of an old event which come forward to a new time and space, but rather the saving content of the former work. Jesus has risen from the dead and He cannot die again. He stands glorious in heaven, showing His wounds to the Father and interceding for us. What comes forward in time is an inrush of saving power, which in some mysterious way touches us in Baptism, the Supper of the Lord, and other sacraments.

Earliest Christianity did not theologize much about the sacraments. But by Augustine's time some reflection began. Augustine drew attention to the fact that a sacrament was a sign or symbol. Contemporary man has an ambiguous attitude toward symbol. He claims it doesn't interest him, though at the same time we can note a crescendo of attention to symbol. Observe a fisherman who renounces any conscious appreciation of symbol. To go fishing he assembles many symbols — a battered hat with fishhooks, special old shoes and pants he always wears. His room looks like a page out of *Field and Stream*. Is such a man oblivious of symbol? On the conscious level, yes, but subconsciously, no.

Everyone's dream life is jam-packed with symbols. Those who feel uncomfortable with the Apocalypse should make a diary of their dream lives and mark the similarity between the imageries. Catechists should remember Augustine's declaration about sacramental symbol because it is essential for pedagogy. The catechist who cannot appreciate symbol will never adequately know how to teach sacraments. Sacramental action is almost entirely in symbolic form. Think of a sacramental symbol as something which speaks. It speaks both its own truth and a theological message. The rushing waters of the Atlantic Ocean speak of power, purity, beauty, and destructiveness. Water is suggestive of life. Bring it into a baptismal context and it speaks too of life, but now of a divine life that drives out sin and makes man a new creature in Christ.

I know of a nun who takes her young students sometimes to a park and settles them by a running stream. She tells them to rest a while quietly by the water. She does not homilize about the qualities of the stream. She just wants them to look at it and hear it. She does not write out a tag that says: "This is a symbol." She allows the symbol to speak for itself. Only then does she begin to speak of the sacrament of Baptism. Studies in comparative religion are refocusing our attention on the great archetypal symbols current in practically every religion. Modern art, poetry, and drama are tireless in using symbols to put across their point. The advertising world would be helpless without symbols for peddling products. For good or ill, symbols are operative today, and catechists would be well advised to become alert to this necessary adjunct for sacramental catechesis.

In the Middle Ages St. Thomas, agreeing with Augustine's theory of the sacramental sign, added that it was an operational sign. The sign accomplished what it signified. Why is Jesus in the chapel? Simply to be there? Or to do something? Do Christians visit the Blessed Sacrament to comfort Christ or to be comforted by Him? There is no point in going there to comfort Him, for He lives in incomparable glory and joy. He is not lonely; humans are. The Eucharistic Bread speaks of consolation, of joy, and of salvation. St. Thomas says the sign of bread is not static, but dynamic. It speaks of Jesus who is the Host at the table of salvation.

But after St. Thomas theologians began to concentrate on the area between sign and effect. They examined endlessly the mode of causality. They took a long and hard look at the bridge that stood between Jesus and the person affected by His action. But they looked so much at this aspect of causality which is shrouded in darkest mystery that they unwittingly forgot the persons involved.

This dry speculation became the staple of theology books, producing generations of clergy and catechists victimized by an impersonal view of the sacraments. How is the heart of a Christian to be moved by demonstrations of modes of causality? Watch young lovers in action. They seem much less interested in how their love occurred than in each other all lost in wonder. This speculation obscured the fundamental notion of sacraments as personal encounters between God and man. Today's theological renewal has recaptured this primary notion and set catechesis on the right road again.

Here are four suggestions for teaching sacraments:

1. Show that their real meaning is the union of the Christian-in-the-Church with the saving action of Christ. Teach sacraments as community affairs, communal events. Sacraments are not private prayers but liturgical events involving the Church. Our sacramental practice had reduced the Mass to a Quaker-style semimystical quiet service; confession to a dark box full of embarrassing intimacies; baptism to a chill lonely service at the door of the church; anointing of the sick to a gasping, lisping last chance at a deathbed. Even holy orders and matrimony, the most obviously social-minded sacraments, were shrouded by an overly individualistic mysticism. In the sacraments the Christian meets Christ, not alone, but within the community.

2. Link each sacrament with the paschal mystery of Jesus. This is easier with baptism and the Eucharist and requires greater efforts with the others. This is accomplished with greater success when each sacrament is taught and practiced within the context of the history of salvation.

3. Explain sacraments by the means which the Church uses to celebrate them. This means not only the basic "matter and form" but also all the words and signs which the Church places for each sacrament. However, since the contemporary context of the sacraments is sometimes overlaid with obscure elements, it is advisable to go back and see an earlier and clearer form. For example, in explaining baptism, follow the rites as existing in the fourth century and commented on by St. Ambrose and St. Cyril of Jerusalem. There the biblical background is more obvious, and catechists can discover the sources which lie behind our present-day rites.

4. Paraliturgies are especially helpful to show the student the style of liturgical procedure, and start situating him for initiation into deeper faith. This assists sacramental pedagogy to escape the accusation of archaeologism or "another class,"

and rather helps students experience involvement in the sacramental idea.

*   *   *

As Jesus was a sign to His generation, the sacraments give His sign power to ours. St. John sees Jesus as not only working signs, but as a sign Himself. Both Jesus and His sacraments must be seen. This demands transparency. This transparency can be obscured by a superstylization of the sacramental sign, or a superabstractionism on the part of the beholder. Historical accretion may have worn the sign of the sacrament thin. Sacramental theology may have made Christian thought too remote from the concreteness of the sign. Today's liturgical revival is restoring the visibility of sacramental action. Today's theological revival is providing the concrete historical foundations for personal, dynamic perception of the sacraments. The happy concursus of both offers the catechist a rich field for an enlightened and fruitful pedagogy.

Chapter 7 Teaching Baptism

> Baptism for babies or believers? The Church of England's canon law decrees that babies should be christened within a fortnight of birth. Parents are prone to stretch the deadline a bit, but now the whole practice is under fire. Three vicars have resigned from the Church of England, announcing that they no longer believe in infant baptism. Three others, with covert support from Low Church vicars, have informed their bishops they will baptize only believing adults (*Time*, January 8, 1965).

If nothing else, this news item is a reminder of the need for bringing the student to an intelligent commitment flowing from the nature of the baptismal rite. It is not likely that infant baptism is going to be abandoned in the Church. Yet our system is a constant reminder of the inverse procedure this entails. The child is saved before he is evangelized. The trap that catechesis can unwittingly fall into is to fail to evangelize the student, to miss shaping his attitudes in such a way that he is gradually and consistently invited, proportionate to his maturity, to make a commitment that is the ultimate demand of baptism. I think catechesis must search for a way of helping students to relive the baptismal event, both to awaken a respect for the importance of this great sacrament of initiation, and to experience the need to make a decision that in all sincerity answers the call of this sacrament.

At the moment the efforts to construct such a catechesis are slowed down by a theological and cultural lag. New studies on baptism are abounding but the process of time is needed for reflection in which the wheat can be separated from the chaff, and the adaptation, pedagogically, can be satisfactorily worked out. The experiments in paraliturgy, the impetus from the Easter vigil, and the reform of the cult obviously are boons to the catechesis of baptism. The architecture of the new churches situating the font in a prominent and honored position, symbolizing the relation between it and the altar, is another bonus for catechesis. The Church's decision to restore the dynamism of the rites in the baptism of converts also aids the cause of catechesis. It is not possible yet to be able to sift out the directions which all these developments lend to the progress of baptismal catechesis.

One constant norm for all sacramental catechesis is to use the details of the Church's prescribed ritual as the fundamental structure for explaining the meaning of the sacrament. The gestures, images, symbols, and words used for sacraments are the normal viable elements by which we can come to know the theological meaning of a given sacrament. But it must be admitted that the contemporary forms are occasionally so obscure that it may be difficult to see the meaning whether in part or in whole. I propose in this chapter to go back to a baptismal ritual of a much earlier age. The spirit of those ceremonies and the openness to biblical interpretation is so rich that it would seem to be a fruitful task and a nudge to the understanding of the possibilities inherent in today's forms. I do not apologize for archaeologism, since this is no commercial for a return to fourth-century ceremonies. My reason is simple. I have found this type of discussion most useful as a way of seeing how we could go about it today.

The following information is garnered from the diary of a wealthy woman, named Aetheria, whose money afforded her the leisure to travel. Her excursions brought her to Jerusalem one spring. Cyril was the bishop, Lent was beginning, and baptismal candidate school was opening. Classes were held at the Martyrium, the ancient and hallowed church of the resurrection, built over the hill upon which Jesus died, and the tomb from which Jesus rose. The details of the Lenten instructions, and the theological asides are taken both from her diary and from the notes of Bishop Cyril's catechesis.

Enrollment Ceremony

On the evening before the first Sunday of Lent, the candidate for baptism went to the Bishop's house to apply for entry into the Christian Church. His application was taken, and he was told to report the next morning at the church. Sunday morning, he came to the church, accompanied by a sponsor. Instructed to take off his shoes, he stood barefoot on an animal cloth rug. The bare feet symbolized slavery, and the rug suggested the tunics of skin which Adam wore after his sin, as signs of his shame. The candidate assumes a symbolic role as a man in sin, subject to the slavery of Satan.

The bishop then quizzed the candidate about his moral life, hoping to determine his acceptability for baptism. The sponsor stood as witness to the credibility of the candidate's affirmations and testimony. If he proved acceptable, then his name was written in the "book of life" and he was admitted to the catechumenate. At this moment a cantor sang the Gospel of Jesus' temptation in the desert, and His triumph over Satan. This is why this Gospel is still read on the first Sunday of Lent.

Forty Days of Catechesis

Aetheria's notes describe the procedure for daily class. It was held each day at the hour of prime — perhaps 7:30 a.m. The sexes were separated. Each class began with an exorcism. Psychologically this reminded the candidates of their need for freedom from Satan. Theologically, the exorcisms gradually freed the candidates from the power of Satan. During the exorcisms the community sang psalms.

The class itself consisted of a reading and explanation of the Bible in both its literal and spiritual meaning. In the latter the catechist aimed at theological and ethical relevance. The teacher presented the Bible as the history of salvation, and isolated the images of Scripture in such a way that they could be seen in the light of the sacraments which the catechumens would soon receive. Generally, in the fifth week, each person was given a copy of the Apostles' Creed and the Our Father. He was told to memorize both texts and prepare for an examination of their meaning. In the sixth week there was a ceremony of the giving of the Gospel. The first chapter of each Gospel was chanted, and then the book was solemnly placed in the hands of each candidate. This reminded him that he will soon live by the Gospel of Jesus.

Final Preparatory Rite

This rite took place on Holy Saturday before the Easter Vigil. It was the ceremony of renouncing Satan and adhering to Christ. The man renounced Satan by facing the west, and with an accompanying gesture of prayer, by reciting the formula, "I renounce the devil and all his works and pomps." The west was the region of darkness, traditionally symbolizing the home of Satan. "Pomps" referred to the grandiose processions which the Romans used in idolatrous worship.

Then he faced the east and proclaimed adherence to Jesus. Ancient peoples believed that paradise was in the east. Jesus rose from the dead at dawn, just as the sun arose in the east. Christians commonly placed a cross on the eastern wall of their homes, and faced east when they prayed. The three great monotheistic religions all had prayer directions: Christians to the east; Jews to Jerusalem; Mohammedans to Mecca.

This brought the candidates to the threshold of the Easter Vigil. Their long preparation culminates in baptism (and confirmation and the Eucharist). At every moment the personal nature of the action has been emphasized. Sacraments are not magic, but require a true personal conversion of heart and a response of faith.

The Rite of Baptism

The candidates have progressed from enrollment and catechesis to the pool. They have been told that the lengthy process is a ritual repetition of the long journey of the Israelites from the bondage of Egypt, across the sea, through the pilgrimage to Sinai, the desert purification (exorcisms) and covenant catechesis, to the promised land, the new paradise of the Church.

Description of the Baptistry

The baptistry was an eight-sided building, modeled after the style of the Roman bathhouses. The symbolism of the eighth day overshadowed its architectural plagiarism. Seven days were the image of earthly time; the eighth day was seen as the symbol of eternity. Sunday became the liturgical commemoration of the eighth day, a memorial of the resurrection, and prophecy of the world to come. Into this eighth day the new Christian comes by baptism. An allusion to this eighth day symbol is found in 1 Peter 3:20: "In the days of Noah, during the building of the ark, eight persons were saved."

The decorations of the baptistry evoked the atmosphere of paradise. Paintings showed the good shepherd surrounded by his flock, in a lush paradise setting of gardens and running streams. Often a deer was seen drinking at the waters. A snake would be wriggling from his mouth. Legendary science taught that when a deer ate a snake, he incurred an intolerable thirst. Hence the deer quenching his thirst in the baptismal waters of paradise symbolized the catechumen quenching his thirst caused by the snake that Adam swallowed.

Strip

Adam first wore clothes only after he had sinned, hence clothing became a symbol of fallen man. Now the candidate takes off this symbol of his slavery to Satan. "Tunics of skin" represent mortality and corruptibility. The stripping is like a return to primitive innocence. The true meaning of the stripping of the garments is the disappearance of shame, proper to man before God, and a recovery of confidence in Him.

Anoint

The candidate prepares now for the final and greatest struggle. He seeks the ultimate moment of freedom from the power of evil. For this he needs strength; hence he rubs himself with oil as does an athlete entering a fierce contest. His impending struggle with the demon is the culmination of the Lenten conflict. Today anointing is only a brief gesture; a little oil is smeared on the chest and between the shoulder blades. Then it was the whole body which was rubbed with oil, so that the catechumen may engage manfully with the diabolic powers of evil resident beneath the baptismal waters. Ancient peoples imagined the watery depths as the home of fearful dragons. The psalms often speak of the leviathans living in the depths of the sea. Satan, the diabolical dragon, resides in the watery deep of the baptismal pool.

The Baptism

The candidate descends into the pool and is completely immersed three times, while the trinitarian formula is recited over him. Paul, in his sixth chapter to the Romans, offers the theology for this action. He explains the theological reality present here, in that the sacramental event acts out the death and resurrection of Jesus. In the redemptive work of Jesus, two things must be considered: the historical fact and the content of saving grace. The historical fact is imitated. The sacramental action symbolizes it. But the content of saving grace allows us a true participation. The two aspects of the sacrament are described perfectly. It is an efficacious symbol of the passion and resurrection, representing the historical deeds physically, and actualizing them spiritually. The burial in the pool corresponds to the entombment of Jesus. The emergence on the other side relates to the resurrection of Christ. The candidate contacts redemption by passing through death to life through the power of Christ made present in the sacramental action.

Clothing

Now the new Christian rises to the other side of the pool. Like Jesus, risen from the dead, he is clothed in a white garment. He is similar to the transfigured Jesus of Thabor and to the Lord of the resurrection. Further, white was the biblical color of priestly vestments (cf. Ex 29:35; Ap 4:1). Perhaps we have here an allusion to the priesthood of all believers.

The Sealing

After the newly baptized has put on the white robe, the bishop seals him with the sign of the cross. Oil is used for this anointing. The Greek term for this marking is *sphragis*. This identified the Christian. As animals were branded, soldiers tattooed, slaves stigmatized, so the Christian was marked to show to whom he belonged. Biblically it was like the mark of Cain (Gn 4:15) or the mark of the elect (Ez 9:4; Ap 7:4) Christologically this sealing signified identification with Jesus, marked with His cross, bearing upon oneself the signs of the Lord Jesus.

As soldiers entered into covenant pacts with their generals and slaves of the gods with their lords by a sealing ceremony, so the Christian through the baptismal sealing concludes his covenant with God. As circumcision sealed the covenant with Abraham, so baptism finalized the covenant of the Christian (cf. Rom 4:11; Eph 1:13). Hence this sealing had two meanings, a static one illustrating identity with Christ, and a dynamic one confirming a covenant with God.

Augustine, in his fight against the Donatists who were

saying that baptism should be repeated many times, declared that the sealing received at baptism was indelible, and could not be removed. Eventually this sealing became known as the baptismal character. This character is the invisible and permanent mark on the soul of the Christian. It is the foundation of the Christian's ability to participate in the Eucharist; in fact, it is a vocation to worship. It is also the ever present capability which enables Christians to be constantly and more deeply assimilated to the attitudes of Jesus.

It was after the sealing that the newly baptized went in procession to the nearby church, where they participated in their first Mass and received the Eucharist for the first time. This was an easy and obvious way to see the link between baptism and the Eucharist.

The catechesis of the Fathers always placed baptism against the background of two exodus events, that of Israel and that of Jesus. To them the sacrament of baptism was a third exodus experience, symbolically repeating the other two and actually making present the saving power of God as evidenced in His Son Jesus. The two exodus images are primary. The Fathers also employed many other scriptural pictures to fill out their teaching on baptism. In the creative waters of Genesis they found the new life that can come to the baptized Christian. The destructive waters of the deluge are a sign of the deliverance from sin as salvation is found in the ark-Church. The cleansing of Naaman the Syrian in the waters of the Jordan is another baptismal image. This was the sort of catechesis congenial to the symbol-minded theologians of the patristic period. They considered themselves true heirs to the typological exegesis already apparent in the prophetic writings of the Old Testament. In a world where symbol was at home, nothing could seem more normal.

What can the modern catechist learn from the fourth-century school? First, that he should teach the sacrament as part of a continuum in the history of salvation, that baptism is one of the mighty acts of God, inaugurated at the exodus, realized in Christ, and continued in the Church. When this is understood, then it becomes clear why the biblical imagery is used, not as a pious decoration, but as truly related to the present event, even more deeply than a heritage is to an heir.

Second, a catechist can learn from this the importance of the personal, especially the dominance of the subjective act of faith and commitment. If the recital of the mighty deeds of God is a necessary evangelical process, indicating the divine initiative and making it operative as the objective thrust of salvation, the personal response is no less imperative, for salvation is an interpersonal affair. It is a dialogue in which the person must give an answer, in freedom, to the divine call.

Third, catechists must look for ways to make the old biblical pictures relevant to the new age. This may mean taking cues from language analysts, depth psychiatrists, and artists and poets. Scriptural exegesis has bravely managed to scrape away much of the cultural crust which hides the biblical symbol, but catechists will still need an assist from the personality sciences and the experts in aesthetics to find a viable form for communication.

These are only some of the possibilities open to baptismal catechesis today. The ecumenical overtones of catechesis will open new and large questions for a divided Christendom. The relation between baptism and ascetics, the Christian's death-life cycle, and the theology of Christian death itself will benefit by this new attention to a sacrament too little considered in the past. Such are some new perspectives and challenges for baptismal catechesis, a dawn, not a sunset, a horizon for new theological adventure.

Chapter 8 ❦ Confirmation

Confirmation is the second of the sacraments of initiation. Modern sacramental procedure obscures this idea which was normative for the early Church. Somehow, through the centuries confirmation receded quietly into the shadows, so that today it is one of the least understood of the sacraments. There are many Christians who never receive confirmation at all. And for those who do get confirmed, there is little or no rationale other than the thought that this makes them soldiers of Christ, fitting them for apostolic action. Very few see any link with baptism and the Eucharist, and almost no one understands confirmation as part of initiation into Christian life. For the majority of children the experience of confirmation is a blur, a rite in which the bishop may frighten them with a question they cannot answer, and then proceeds expertly and hastily to brush some oil against their foreheads as he pats the side of their face.

Neither liturgists nor theologians seem confident yet about the present role of confirmation, nor its exact theological dimension. A thorough, critical history of the sacrament has yet to be written. But there is no doubt that we can anticipate that the sacrament of confirmation will share in the general theological and liturgical renewal. Meanwhile, catechists will have to be patient until the research is done and published. It is with this slight pessimistic reserve that I offer a few ideas about the sacrament that may be serviceable for modern catechesis.

Confirmation is in a particular way a sacrament which involves a special action of the Holy Spirit. This sacrament is often popularly called the Christian's Pentecost. So it is imperative that catechists have a basic grasp of the work of the Holy Spirit as explained from the biblical perspective. Since I have already done this in the chapter on the Spirit, I feel no need to repeat those ideas here. But I do want to discuss some particular relationships between the action of the Spirit as manifested in the New Testament and the sacraments of baptism and confirmation.

Following the first rite of Christian initiation, baptizing, a seal is placed upon it (cf. Eph 1:14; 4:30). Generally it was an anointing and a laying on of hands. The anointing aspect seems to indicate the deputation to a priestly and kingly role in the Church, priestly insofar as the person is oriented to the sacrifice of the Church, kingly inasmuch as the Christian is awarded the potential of leadership in the community. Some have argued that confirmation is a baptism of the Spirit in contrast to the mere baptism of water in the first instance. This is normally discredited in many scholarly circles. The issue is not sufficiently clear to allow catechists to make a firm decision one way or another. The norm in this case will be the current practice of the Church which sees baptism and confirmation as two separate sacraments, the Holy Spirit imparted in both, and the two as a continuum in the rite of initiation.

Nevertheless, attention is so strongly focused on the Holy Spirit in confirmation that we cannot ignore this idea, and we must search for reasons why. In the Bible the Spirit is generally contrasted with the flesh. Flesh does not simply mean body, but a whole human being, soul and body with its attendant physical phenomena and emotional attributes. But flesh is the human person caught in the web of the human condition, enshrouded by the chaos of an evil world, and shorn of hope for redemption by self-determination. The flesh signifies man cut off from God, but in position for atonement, for reconciliation with the redemptive power of the Lord.

When Jesus rose from the dead He promised to send the Spirit as witness to the new Christian of the meaning of salvation. By the Spirit, Christ intended to awaken in Christians a personal identification with His teachings and deeds. The flesh must give way to the life of the Spirit. Hence the spiritual life is a dialogue between the Christian and the Holy Spirit. It is by the continuous and valid interrelation of the Christian to the Spirit that gradually an identification with Christ is achieved. The sacrament of confirmation is a witness of this phenomenon, because of its Pentecostal quality and prophetlike anointing. I mentioned above that the anointing may have reflected an allusion to the kingly and priestly roles of the Christian, but I believe there is a strong element of prophecy symbolized.

The New Testament constantly links the work of the Spirit with prophetic work. The baptism of Jesus at the Jordan is much less a priestly ordination than it is a prophetic investiture. How often Jesus is taken from the beaten path by the charism of the Spirit. How frequently formalized situations in the life of Paul or Peter and the others are interrupted as the Spirit intervenes. The Bible clearly distinguishes institutional religion from the unforeseen inrush of the Spirit who temporarily diverts history, causing what seems to be a mutation or, better, a growth in the union between God and His people. This does not imply that one is better than the other. For example, the role of the priesthood in the Old Testament seems to be (besides its fundamental task of mediatorship) a conservative and institutionalizing factor.

It is the clergy who reverently preserve the traditions of the Fathers, the oracles of the prophets, and the enlightened decisions of the kings. The clergy offer that sense of stability, continuity and symmetry which mediates the course of sacred history through the ages. Paul's memorable charge to Timothy — "Guard the deposit of faith" — is the general rubric for priestly action. But without any prejudice to this obviously necessary role, the Bible equally extols the quality of charism, of spontaneous prophecy in the Church. This is why John the Baptist was so wildly acclaimed along the banks of the

Jordan, so much so that all Jerusalem and Judea went out to see and hear him. It had been four centuries since the voice of prophecy had rung on the air and stones of the Holy Land.

The people of the Bible had a deep respect for prophecy and a built-in sensitivity to its value. They rated charismatic gifts highly while never discounting the practical necessity of conserving the insights in an established community. The sacrament of confirmation is a sacrament of prophecy, in that the Christian has a special encounter with the Holy Spirit who spoke through the prophets. Confirmation is a witness to Christians that the Church continues the charismatic traditions extolled in Bible times. The New Testament links the gift of the Spirit with that of prophecy. "And when Paul laid his hands upon them, the Holy Spirit came on them; and they spoke with tongues and prophesied" (Acts 19:6). I am using the term "prophecy" in the sense of spontaneous and incisive faith declarations which reflect the divine view of historical circumstances, as well as courageous personal willingness to witness the consequences in their lives. Prophecy is not a tricky prediction process, pretending to have an inside line with God, but rather a dual sensitivity to the godly view of history and to the significance of particular human events.

Confirmation is the sacrament which guarantees that the voice of prophecy will not die out in the Church. The clerical establishment insures the institutionalizing of prophetic utterance, and with age-old wisdom presides at the birth of a new utterance, testing its validity, mindful of the biblical admonition to still the voice of the false prophets, and the pledge of the Spirit to help her be a discerner of spirits. If baptism is an incorporation into the establishment, confirmation is an investiture of spiritual sensitivity to the correctives any historical establishment may need, and a vision to the new directions wherein it should develop. Confirmation is a sacrament that helps the bones of the Church to awake to new life, the eyes dimmed by age to flash with new color, the strength stiffened by past success, accepted and enshrined, to flex again with new power.

Confirmation is a sacrament of purification that spurs Christian witness to accept the pains of growth and renewal. It moves men to stand bravely in the sight of princes and kings, to rejoice in the privilege of suffering for the Church, even when the Church herself may be the protagonist of the pain, for Christ may place the cross wherever He wishes. The idea of charismatic gift can romantically appear as an adventure in dreamlike freedom in which the Christian witness haughtily stands outside the establishment, waving an admonishing finger, secure in its inner certainty, and patronizing the Church Catholic. Such a view of prophecy has no support in Scripture, which time and time again pictures the stoning of the prophets. They are always men throroughly embroiled in the event of their times. They are not so much men apart, as they are men who willingly step into the nexus of tension, supporting its survival, crucified by its intolerable burden, but forever pledged to fidelity to the pledged witness.

Though confirmation is the vocation to prophecy, it by no means supplies authentic credentials for identifying a real expression of the charism. Jesus said that the Spirit will breathe where He wills; hence, like the wind, His presence has a certain unpredictability about it. The Pentecosts of the Church are intermittent, and cannot be plotted with mathematical assurance. The ultimate test of the validity of prophetic witness is the judgment of the Christian community in whom is the fullness of the Spirit's voice.

All these remarks may have the flavor of unreality about them, and may seem to reduce confirmation to a sacrament of occasional value. It can portray confirmation as an emergency sacrament, somewhat like the anointing of the sick, summoned by the Church to minister to an historical crisis, but reduced to a whisper in periods of calm. The life of an individual Christian does not always move in such dramatic arenas, nor is it always privileged to function in the face of shattering experience. But in a lower key, Christian living does confront a continuity of human experiences that never escapes need for the Spirit-inspired deed. Confirmation gives Christians, on whatever level of historical tragedy or vacuity, the necessary sensitivity to preceive in a godly way, and witness within the shadow of the cross.

There is a lively debate abroad as to when the sacrament should be received. One school favors reception before First Communion. I would call it the theological school. Proceeding from the principle of God's initiative they affirm that even the youngest child can benefit from the charism of the Spirit, and, in fact, stands in need of it. Why deny the child the earliest possible benefits of confirmation in which the Spirit begins to work strongly and sweetly in the child's soul? Furthermore, they affirm that confirmation is one of the sacraments of initiation into the Christian life, hence it seems illogical to wait another ten years to permit the child to be confirmed. Their viewpoint stands within the framework of the transcendent God and the idea of religion as a structure of grace. God comes to the child in His gracious majesty and does what He has always done in sacred history — continues His work of salvation.

The other school commits itself to teen-age confirmation. I would call it the psychological school. Their arguments function within the shadow of an immanent God and the sovereign beauty of human freedom. Their concern is not so much with the divine initiative (which they affirm absolutely), but with the phenomenon of response. They argue that the child has already received three sacraments (baptism, the Eucharist, and penance) at so early an age that he was scarcely aware of what was happening, and when his response structure was so weak that it is impossible to gauge any adequacy. They do not reject an early sacramental life for the child, they only plead that at least one of the sacraments of initiation be held in abeyance until the child has reached a degree of maturity which involves true decision-making. They agree that confirmation is, indeed, the true complement to baptism, but they want to widen the time continuum between them.

One factor is strongly on their side, namely, the current practice of the Church, which does separate confirmation from baptism by at least ten to fifteen years. Further, as the new look in catechesis understands its role as a commitment-producing function, it would like to situate confirmation as the landmark sacrament. To them confirmation is the sign of achievement. It is the end product of years of arduous effort in which catechesis labored to proportion the Christian message to the dynamics of decision in the child, gradually evoking truer and more authentic choices, and bringing him at the crest of his religious destiny to make the firm and final choice for Christ. Confirmation becomes the dramatic seal of the work begun in baptism, only now done in the full light of day, proceeding from an enlightened conscience and a well-tested power of decision.

Both schools of thought have attractive features, the one reflecting the surge of theological insight into the sacraments as the work of God, and the other influenced by the dynamics current in the personality sciences. The debate has a long way to go, and it is too soon to see the outcome. Who knows, perhaps a third school may arise? Who can predict what ordinary Church procedure may do to influence the debate? Since the research monographs available are slight, much theological conversation is still needed.

In the meantime the catechists must work with the theological insights of the present and the current practice in the community. I hope that the general leads given in this chapter may furnish a mood for thought about confirmation and a thirst for deeper penetration into the problem. The Spirit of prophecy is abroad in the Church today. I am certain He will be active in bringing forth the treasures of His sacrament to rejoice the Church, temper the Christian, and enliven Christian testimony.

Chapter 9 ❦ The Eucharist

Few miracles impressed the people of the Gospel more than the miracle of the loaves. All the Gospels tell the story and two of them tell it twice. They remember it because of its extraordinary eucharistic significance. In a lonely spot by the sea, Jesus anticipated the messianic banquet foretold in the Old Testament as the sign of the saving day of the Lord. The loave miracles of those nights by the sea are told in terms of the Eucharist. In Mark's Gospel the shape of the Eucharist is clear. Jesus takes the bread, blesses it, breaks it, distributes it. The memory of the Eucharist was of central concern to primitive Christianity.

The texts of institution all vary slightly. We have five in all, four in Scripture, and the one used in our present-day Mass. Each text represents a refinement of the core memory by several of the dominant Christian communities of the infant Church. Form critics such as Jeremias and Lietzmann attempt to sort out the sources and comparative antiquity of each text, but the subject is still open.

The Eucharist is a witness. It witnesses, for example, all the meals that Jesus ever ate. Those who think of the Eucharist exclusively as a sacrifice are not prepared to view it as a meal. Not many Christians think of the Eucharist as primarily a meal, even though this is fundamental in the scriptural accounts. It stands for the communion of Christ and His friends at the fellowship of the table. The Eucharist witnesses the meals Jesus ate with His family, the Apostles, and the crowds on those great guest nights by the lake. It recalls the Last Supper, the evening at Emmaus, and the Galilean feast during one of His postresurrection experiences.

Catechists must be sensitive to the symbolism of a meal.

91

Perhaps only the sexual symbol is superior on the natural level to illustrate the union that must exist between men. The warmth of a friendly meal taken together is a model and sign of human communion. Eating together is a holy act as humans face one another and are nourished by the same bread and drink. Whenever Jesus sat at table He generally was in union with those present. Wisely He chose the meal as the enduring sign of His wish always to be in union with humanity — a union that is personal, loving, and redemptive.

The Eucharist is a witness to the death of Christ. Paul wrote to the Corinthians that every time they ate the bread and drank of the cup they announced the death of the Lord until He comes. The most ancient fragment of the Gospel record is the story of the death and resurrection of Jesus. It is most likely that in the first Eucharists the liturgical recitation was invariably the passion-resurrection narrative. Hence each Eucharist is a showing forth of the death of the Lord. The gradual for the feast of the Lord's Supper on Holy Thursday sings of the death of Jesus. Jesus is obedient unto death.

An indication of the antiquity of the passion narrative can be derived from a clue in St. John's Gospel. Written many years after the synoptics, John writes in an independent spirit. His account rearranges much of the early material, centers itself around liturgical and symbolic motifs and seems more mystical than the synoptic record. But his account of the passion suddenly brings him into line with the earlier stories. John's passion, while it has different prodigy stories and certain additions, is essentially the same as the synoptic one. Apparently John did not wish to tamper with the archives at Ephesus which insured the liturgical tradition of that town. The eucharistic community at Ephesus had long since preserved their text showing forth the death of the Lord. This was done with a true sense of liturgical memory as it made present for the eschatological congregation the saving power of the death of the Lord, evangelically through the word and sacramentally through the meal.

The Eucharist is more than an obituary. It is not a morbid funeral feast. It is the witness of Christ's resurrection and as such it is a meal of joy. I have a feeling that the prevailing catechesis of the Eucharist lies too much within Calvary's shadow, overemphasizing the death of Christ, and that this catechesis imperceptibly symbolizes the liturgic state of liturgy in pre-Council days. Many Christians do not approach the Eucharist with joy, visibly moved by the love feast. The apostolic Christian communities "broke their bread at home, and did take their food with gladness, singleness of heart, praising God" (Acts 2:46).

How many Sunday-morning congregations are taking their Food with gladness? From how many altars in this country does a living Christ shine forth? For how many Christians is the Eucharist the celebration of the resurrection. Jesus is not dead, He is alive. Catechesis must never forget this.

The Real Presence

It may be useful to speak of Jesus present to the Eucharist as well as in it. Thinking of Christ exclusively in terms of being in the Eucharist can result in a "container complex." Christ is not boxed in by the Eucharist, just as the Holy Spirit is not caged in by the bodily dimensions of the Christian. No human or natural space is the measure of God's might and mystery.

There are many kinds of presence. The most basic is spatial-physical presence. Spatial presence means you are dynamically repelling all the forces which would dislodge you from whatever space you occupy. Second, there is extended spatial presence. When a boy throws a rock through a window, he becomes present to the shattered glass and responsible for its breakage. When America urges Saturn V off the launching pad and sends it to the moon, this will be extended spatial presence.

Yet there is a higher form of presence, namely, personal presence. This happens when one touches the personal awareness of another, and possibly influences the consciousness and affectivity of the other. This is a superior form of presence because it is interpersonal. It is not a physical displacement, but an interior encounter. The analogy of the soul's presence to the body may be of some assistance. We know that if we lose a finger or another limb, the soul is not lost. The soul is not only present in the body, but toward the body, dynamically related to it to bring vitality. The soul is in a position toward the flesh, energizing it and thoroughly united to it in the most conceivably intimate union.

When we think of the real presence of Jesus in the Eucharist, the above ideas of personal presence and the analogy of the dynamic relation of soul to body could enrich and enliven our viewpoint. Such a view quickens the speech of the eucharistic Bread. Here is a motion toward, someone poised to do something, rather than the still white Host that is the staple of popular devotion, characterized by the tabernacled-prisoner thesis.

Jesus is a presence toward as well as a presence in. The Holy Spirit's presence toward the Christian describes his effort to remain in fruitful, saving dialogue. He is doing something to the Christian. In turn the eucharistic Jesus is in a vital posture toward the Christian, reaching out to affect all Christians with His love, concern, and salvation power. The Eucharist, then, is a sign of Jesus thrust into the awareness of Christians to save them, change them, and bring them joy.

A Sign of Unity

The Eucharist is a sign of the unity of the Church, in fact a sign of the Church itself. It may be useful to distinguish between a eucharistic and a universal ecclesiology. The early Christian dioceses found their highest sense of unity in the celebration of the Eucharist. The focal point of the diocese was the celebration of the Supper of the Lord. It was this which drew Christians together and gave them their identification as members of the Church. They were a eucharistic community. A theology of such a community could fairly be termed a eucharistic ecclesiology.

The expansion of the Church in the fourth century, its gradual identification with the cultural forms of the Roman empire, resulted in an adaptation, for practical reasons, of the organizational patterns of the imperial city. This affinity with the organizational structure of the political form assisted the Church to assume a procedure for unity in the international sphere. Theologians were able to shape this into a universal ecclesiology. Magnificent as this is, it tends to make us lose sight of the family-style ecclesiology which found expression in the diocesan Eucharist.

The unifying factor for Christians is the ability to partake of the Bread of Life. They may not always be aware of it, but this does not make it any the less true.

Origen of Alexandria has a memorable teaching on this subject. For him every symbol points to something beyond itself. When talking about the real presence of Jesus he maintains that it is possible to speak of intensity of realness. It is possible to be more real. Jesus of Galilee was real. He points to the Gospel which carries His reality into history. His presence in the living word can seem more real to us than the confining presence of an ancient time and space. But the scriptural word points beyond itself to the sacrament. The Eucharist is a more real presence of Jesus than is the biblical passage. To hold the Bible in one hand and the Host in another would quickly show us in which case Jesus seems more real.

Yet the Eucharist too points beyond itself, namely, to the Church. It is in the community of Christians joined in love where Christ achieves His most dynamic and real presence in the world. Just as the sign of a person seems more real than the sign of bread, so the assembly of agape-bound Christians is a more credible parousia of Christ than the bread. This is all stated with no sense of slight, but with the reverent perception of one of the Church's greatest theologians. The

Eucharist is not terminal. Even the body of Christians themselves is not terminal, for they should manifest a Christ of glory who one day will be blindingly clear to all those who have been faithful.

The Eucharist Produces Unity

The Eucharist produces the Church. The Church is more fully Church after each celebration of the Supper of the Lord. The Church is always in growth, dynamically realizing her own potentiality. It is the special power of the Eucharist to advance the intensity of the Church's life and existence. The bond of community in classrooms, parishes, rectories, convents, monasteries, and family circles takes its thrust from the power of the Eucharist.

Eucharist as Sacrifice

When Jesus entered the upper room He did so as a Jew, with the mentality of an Israelite about to celebrate the Passover. The chief food for the supper was the paschal lamb. The problem is to make the lamb holy, and hence to have sacrifice. What is the lamb before it is holy? It is profane, as yet not totally offered to the Lord. The lamb was in the flock, in the world of profane. Take him now, set him apart from the flock, gradually prepare him to enter the realm of the holy. Kill the lamb. This does not make him holy, but it does make him ready for the transition to the world of the holy. The butchering process is not sacrifice. A rabbi is not always needed, nor is there a necessary liturgical formula accompanying the immolation.

The divine instrument of sanctification in Scripture is normally fire. The divine fire comes from heaven to make things holy. Fire rushes from heaven on the plains of Carmel to make holy the offerings of Elijah. Of course not every fire comes directly from God, but these events are archetypal to show the symbolic power of fire in a sacrificial act. At a Passover meal when the lamb has been brought as far from the world of the profane as men can bring it, then fire is applied, i.e., God's transforming power appears and He takes the lamb unto Himself. Fire goes into the fat, making a sweet smell. God as a spiritual Being could not eat the lamb, but He could inhale its sweetness. "And when the Lord smelled the pleasing odor (of Noah's lamb), he said in his heart: 'I will never again curse the ground because of man'" (Gn 8:21). The sweetness of the transformed lamb rises to God and He accepts it making it holy. Afterward the members of the table commune in the holy lamb — God's meat. In so doing they are made holy by partaking of God's food. This communing must correspond to their inner wish to move themselves away from the profane also into the world of the holy. They must offer themselves to God and await His transforming action. The sacrifice in this case is a meal, and it is a sacrifice because it is a meal.

On Holy Thursday night at the Passover meal, Jesus took two existing ceremonies and transposed and transformed them into signs of a new covenant. The ceremony called for a blessing of the bread and the cup, one preceding, the other succeeding the eating of the passover lamb, sign of the old covenant. Remember that this meal was strictly ritualized. All those present had seen this meal dozens of times and knew exactly what to expect, and with the reverent conservatism of the deeply religious, they did not want anything changed.

On that great night there was an *aggiornamento*, a change in the liturgy, but a change far more profound than liturgical renewal. Christ took the bread and blessed it, that is, He pressed His hand upon it, pouring into it His divine vitality. His hand became the transforming fire bringing this bread from the profane into the utterest holiness. Then that those observing might realize the change, He spoke new words. "Take and eat, this is I — My Body." Then they ate the lamb, and the time came for blessing the cup. He took the cup, blessed it, and gave them to drink. "Here drink of this, for this is My Life — My Blood." And to make sure there would be no mistake that a great change was occurring, He added, "of the new and eternal covenant. This is My life of the new covenant." By this new blessing of the bread and the cup, Jesus established a new paschal meal. Like the Passover meal of old, it was a sacrifice, precisely because it was a meal. When Jesus said "new covenant" the Apostles could understand Him in terms of Jeremiah's prediction that one day God would visit His people and establish a new covenant bond. "Behold the days are coming when I will make a new covenant with the house of Israel" (Jer 31:31 ff.).

The blood served as a sealing of the new covenant. At Mount Sinai, after the giving of the Torah and the establishment of the first covenant, Moses took a basin of lamb's blood, representing God's life, sprinkled some on the altar and the rest on the people. Thus the treaty was sealed in the blood of the lamb. Hence the cup in the Mass seals the covenant of the new dispensation.

Christ begins in earnest His paschal action in the upper room. He begins the journey that will take Him through the dark waters of death and ultimately to glory at His Father's right hand. As Jesus walks into the upper room the passion-resurrection mystery begins. Here originates the first setting apart from the profane, proceeding relentlessly onward through the trial, via dolorosa, cross, burial, resurrection, and sending of Spirit. Christ's march into the halls of death is ultimate removal from the profane. The Father accepts the offered body of His Son, transforms it from the lowliness of death into the likeness of glory. It is better now than before, for it is holy — totally belonging to the Father and forever free from the power of the profane. In sacrifice it is not the immolation that is all important so much as the transition to holiness, the transformation to the holy.

Catechesis has concentrated too much on the immolative aspect of sacrifice to the exclusion of transition and transformation. Sacrifice is a passage — a passover. It is a going

from something worse to something better. The purely immolative view is static and tends to cancel out the idea of
movement to something better. Such an approach is negative,
prone to be absorbed in the painful crisis of death to the exclusion of joyful resurrection. Sacrifice means change and
transformation from the profane to the holy.

In the Supper of the Lord the priest becomes the divine
fire, God's instrument of transformation whereby a change
takes place at the words of institution. The Offertory of the
Mass occurs after the consecration as the priest in union
with the worshiping community offers the risen body of
Christ to our Father: "Wherefore, we, being mindful of the
blessed passion, resurrection and ascension of Jesus, now offer
you, O Father, the perfect, holy, and pure gift." The worshipers, having come apart from the profane into the holy
space of the church, now have the risen Jesus in their midst,
and have pleased the Father by the offering of the body of
His Son. Now they await the event of entering into holiness
themselves. Through Communion the divine fire touches each
of the worshipers and makes them holy. Christ's body was
offered and accepted by the Father. The community in union
with Him offered themselves. The Communion is the sign
of the Father's acceptance of the worshipers, and the power
by which He makes them holy. This is the sacrificial action
wherein God is praised by the congregation, which blending
its accents with the canticle of Jesus, is made holy by God's
action in the Eucharist.

When we speak of the Eucharist transforming the Christian
we must ask in what does this transformation consist? The
answer is found in considering the action of Christ in the
whole complex of events that make up the paschal mystery,
especially from the upper room to the sending of the Spirit.
In all these events the one abiding feature is the attitude
which Jesus maintained, namely, obedience to His Father
through a perfect Self-giving. The perfect posture of Christ
is that of Self-offering even to death. This decision to die,

stemming from Christ's dedicated love of His Father, has never disappeared. He never revoked that decision, and the attitude of Self-giving which prompted it abides forever. The death has disappeared, but the decision has not.

It is this attitude of Jesus which you encounter in the sacrament. He comes to every Christian with the dominant attitude which He had toward His Father during His earthly existence. That is what He brings to you *His own attitude toward God* as He reaches into you to change your consciousness and affectivity. Never is this done more deeply and effectively than in the Eucharist. As Jesus moved toward the culmination of His existence. His life was like a crescendo which reached its height in the triumphant liturgical proclamation on the cross when He said, "*Consummatum est.*" Being made holy means transformation to the Holy One of Israel. Rarely is this more true than at the eucharistic Sacrifice.

Hence the magnificent meaning of the Supper of the Lord. Christ enters the deepest awarenesses of the Christian to conform him to the wishes of the Father. This is to be "in Christ Jesus."

Some Ideas on Presentation

1. Show the meaning of the Eucharist in the history of salvation. This means an explanation of the history of the paschal meal, and its reference to the event of the exodus. Explain the signs of bread, wine, lamb, and meal. Show how this meal is a sacrifice. Teach Jesus as oriented toward His hour. He gravitates toward Jerusalem. Draw attention to the many meals of Jesus, the intimate ones with His Apostles and the great feedings by the lake. Note the parables of the supper and the wedding feasts. Teach the Last Supper as similar but superior to the paschal meal. It is a sign of the new alliance. Use the sermon on the bread of life (Jn 6) and the discourse at the Last Supper to discover the *inner mind* of

Jesus about the Eucharist. Ask what He demands of us from this mystery.

2. Explain the liturgy of the Mass, the meaning of the different parts, their contrasts and values. Using Jungmann's *Mass of the Roman Rite*, show your students the evolution of the Mass from the simple meal of the upper room through the first primitive liturgies, the medieval accretions, the fixation at Trent, and the possibilities opened up by the liturgical constitution of the Second Vatican Council. Read *Worship* magazine, which continues to explore the deeper theological dimensions of liturgy.

3. Doctrinal explanations will demand that you teach the Eucharist as: (a) witness to history; (b) the Christian Passover; (c) an ecclesial sacrament; (d) a sacrifice. You must be ready to show Christians how to die with Christ as part of the commitment implicit in the Eucharist. This means an identification with Christ's attitude of obedience and dedication to death, expressed in today's crisis of faith in the face of the human condition. Teach the baptismal character as a power that entitles Christians to participate in the Eucharist and to be assimilated to the attitudes of Jesus.

4. Be up to date on the developments in the liturgical movement. Always help people to participate meaningfully in the Eucharist. Eucharistic catechesis is one of the noblest works entrusted to any catechist. Few are more challenging; few are more satisfying. Bring God's family to its greatest meal with an enlightened faith, and a willing heart. God will do the rest.

Chapter 10 ✠ A Catechesis
of the Mass*

Theology manuals, spiritual treatises, and sermon books display mild schizophrenia in their approach to the Eucharist. Generally they pursue an either/or or, at best, an either/and setup. Sacrament and sacrifice emerge as the two basic categories for studying the Eucharist. I suggest that a broader division be made, not hoping to fragment the Eucharist further, but rather to guarantee a greater adhesiveness and integrity than was possible in the old distinction, while at the same time retaining the luxuriant riches inherent in the newer insights. Each of the seven topics which follow must be considered avenues that are broad and long, finding only an initial thrust in this chapter.

The Mass Is Assembly

Israel was the community of those who covenanted with God at Sinai. It was a called-community, not one which came together by the consent of the members. The cohesiveness of Israel was the result of a divine vocation and summons. Called into being by God's word, this community was holy and priestly for it mediated the cry of sinful man to God's throne of mercy and bore the light of His glory into a world darkened by idolatry.

So also is the Church, the new Israel, when it gathers for worship. The Christian people do not group for Mass by reason of obligation so much as by the call of God.

It is He who has summoned the worshipers to His altar. "Come to the wedding" is the accent proceeding from God.

---

* This chapter appeared in *The American Ecclesiastical Review*, June, 1965. Reprinted with permission.

The Christian assembly exists by reason of invitation, not by obligation, for God always addresses Himself to the freedom He has placed in the heart of man. The liturgical community cannot tolerate selfish individualism at the moment of worship. Too often the people gathered for Mass have seemed like the dry bones in Ezekiel. It is necessary for God to breathe His Spirit over them and quicken them to life in order to form a man — the Christ who can truly praise the Father.

The sign of the bread and wine is a symbol which speaks of the unity of the assembly, and furthermore produces this assembly. It is not only a showing forth of the Church, but also the power of Jesus deepening the union of His People. Today's great liturgical challenge is to restore the notion and experience of the worshiping community which considers itself called and formed by the breath of God which is His Spirit.

The Mass Is Work

It is evident that the Mass is the work of Christ, but it is necessary to state that the Mass is also the work of the Christian people. The very word "liturgy" derives from a Greek term that implies the work of the people. In fact the liturgy on earth is impossible without the people's involvement.

Since the Mass is work, effort must be visible within the assembly. Worship is no easy task when undertaken seriously. At the end of each liturgical service the people should be somewhat weary, not from boredom, but from the hard work resulting from their contribution. True, the people should also experience an exhilaration because of their encounter with God on the holy ground of worship. Hence the liturgical experience, when well done, effects a weary exhilaration.

Jesus does not act apart from His sacrificing Church. The Epistle to the Hebrews describes the liturgy in heaven with Jesus, the high priest, showing His wounds to the Father and interceding for us. The liturgy on earth is not only a participation in this heavenly glory, and not only the act of the head, Jesus, but also the action of the people. Jesus doesn't need this liturgy; we do.

Hence the need to work, to make each Mass a creative effort of the people. The Mass is not just the work of the priest or choirmaster. If so, then the Mass becomes a purely social drill. In this age of a newly recovered response to the role of the Spirit, the working Christian assembly should learn how to balance the rigidity of rubrics with the style of oral tradition. This is not a plea for the abolition of rubrics, which would result in chaos, but rather a recognition of the quickening of the Spirit, breathing a creative life into the age-old forms. It is not a crumbling of walls so much as a transposition of theme.

Today's task is to create a living liturgy. This calls for a working assembly of worshipers awakened to a positive and involving vocation.

The Mass Is Word

God creates by His word. In Genesis He says, "Let there be light," and light appears. Jesus tells cripples to walk and they dance in the streets. Peter sends the word of salvation over the crowd at Pentecost square and three thousand enter into the new creation which is the Church. In every Mass the creative word of God is pronounced over the assembly in order to make them more fully the Church.

Jesus began His mission by standing on Jordan's bank and announcing that the reign of God had finally come. It was good news. Christ by these words began to evangelize the world, asking those who would surrender to Him to change from their old ways and accept His salvation. In the word service of the Fore-Mass Jesus still retains the posture of Jordan's bank sending out His challenge to the assembly to change, hear the good news, and submit to His saving action.

The word is a sword of judgment that reaches into the heart of the community and urges deeper commitment or else demands the honesty of rejection. The word should proceed with such intensity that no one can remain indifferent to it. Each gathering of the liturgical community is an event of judgment or salvation.

Since no one word service could fully express the mystery of Jesus, it is necessary that there be a progressive unfolding of texts over the course of the Church year. In this way the Christian has the chance to assimilate in a progressive and rhythmic way the rich overtones of the mystery of Jesus.

Hence the word service is creative, evangelical, saving, and contemplative. Such perspectives restore the dignity and purposefulness of the position of the word as Mass.

The Mass Is Pasch

The Mass is the Christian Passover. God commanded a Passover meal and the celebration of the unleavened bread to serve as a memorial of the liberation from Egypt (cf. Ex 12:14–13:8). When Paul recites the institution of the Eucharist in First Corinthians 11:24 and focuses attention on the "Do this in memory of me," he is saying that Jesus institutes a new memorial, a new pasch, delivering the new Israel from sin and death.

It is clear Jesus intended the symbolism of the Passover meal to be applied to the Mass. The bread of the Christian Passover is like the unleavened bread of the Jews, a memorial of salvation. Christ consciously identifies Himself with the paschal lamb, replacing it and becoming the new body-lamb which takes away the sins of the world. It is no accident that He ordered His farewell meal to take place at Passover time. Jesus gathered three great symbols around the final meal in the upper room to show that His new covenant should abide in terms of the old Passover. The unleavened bread, the paschal lamb, and the Passover feast surround His presentation of the bread and wine as the food and drink of the new memorial.

The early Church saw the Eucharist always in terms of the

Passover theology. Jesus died and rose at Passover time. Nothing could be more meaningful to a Jewish Christian in the early days of the Church.

The Mass is pasch. This is the clear will of Christ. He taught this interpretation. He deliberately went to Jerusalem at Passover time. He was the answer to Isaac's plaintiff cry: "Who shall provide the lamb?" Jesus through the words of institution at the Last Supper utters the reverent answer: "I am the lamb, who takes away the sins of the world." This is a new exodus, not from physical slavery, but from the bondage of the Prince of Darkness.

The Mass Is Sacrifice

Jesus entered the upper room for the Last Supper with the consciousness and culture of a Jew of His time. This means that He and everyone present knew that the meal about to be eaten would be a sacrifice. A lamb had been taken from the world of the profane and would be made holy. It was not so much the killing that made it holy as it was the fire. Fire is the biblical sign of God's transforming power. God enters by fire into the fat of the lamb producing the sweet savor. Abel's sacrifice was acceptable for the sweet savor rose to God, and in the anthropomorphic sense, God could partake of it. Cain's smoke did not rise. An alliance is formed because men do not want a distant God. If God is distant then life is cut off.

In the paschal meal, the lamb was the sign of the alliance. The killing and immolation of the lamb was not of primary importance. What was important was the action of the fire which transformed the lamb. Transformation, not immolation, was the compelling issue in sacrifice. Fire (figuratively) descends from God and transforms the lamb into a savor pleasing to Him.

Keep the whole paschal feast in mind, noting that the atmosphere of covenant-alliance dominates. The meal is not just incidental; it is the sacrificial action. In taking the bread and the cup, in such an atmosphere, Jesus by His new creative words institutes the sacrifice of the new covenant. What He did by sign at the table He acts out in the parablelike deeds of His final day on earth.

In the upper room Jesus the lamb leaves the place of exile, the world of the profane, and begins His journey through the waters of death. By the transforming power of His Father, His body is changed into the flesh of the resurrection. His journey begins at the Last Supper and He is ultimately set apart from the profane at Calvary when He passes out of our temporal existence. Sacrifice means to make holy. This is a single action that takes place in two phases. Negatively, it involves a separation from the profane; positively, it calls for a transformation that means an integration into the life of the holy. The supper, the trial, and the cross are the scenes of the separation from the profane; the resurrection is the event of transformation. The supper, the cross, and the resurrection from one mystery.

In the Mass we bring ourselves and the bread and wine and set all apart from the world of the profane. The priest is the divine fire whereby the bread and wine are transformed and made holy, bringing into our presence the most holy body of Jesus. We offer Him to our Father as the most pleasing sacrifice of praise. In the Communion Jesus takes us and offers us to the Father and in accepting our separation from the profane applies to us the fire of transforming love making us holy and acceptable to the Father. We eat together that God may no longer be distant from us, nor cut us off from life. We gather at this table to experience a transformation into the holy.

Practically speaking this means approaching the Mass-Sacrifice with the same inner awareness and attitude which Jesus had on His way to the cross. He was surrendered to His Father's will in the context of the life and death experience that lay before Him. We, too, approach the table with an inner acceptance of the concrete situation of our life, especially as it may involve the conflicts and tensions of modern existence. Jesus transforms us that we may confront our daily existence in progressive identification with His awareness and attitude toward it.

The Mass, then, is a sacrificial meal that transforms, rather than destroys us. It is a transfiguration event, anticipating the final transformation in our resurrection.

The Mass Is Meal

We have looked at the altar as the rock of sacrifice so long that we seldom recall that the Mass is meal as well. Paul says: "Is it not the supper of the Lord that you eat?" (1 Cor 11:20). That final banquet recalls the days when Jesus broke bread for His disciples in Galilee. It remembers the lakeside meals when Jesus broke bread on those great guest nights when He spoke of bread from heaven.

Our Mass today is the supper of the Lord, for the Host of Galilee, Capernaum, and Jerusalem still stands at our table.

Sometimes it is hard to see the signs. Note how we have stylized the meal beyond recognition:

> altar . . . table
> priest . . . servant
> host . . . bread
> chalice . . . cup
> paten . . . plate
> Mass . . . supper of the Lord
> church building . . . home

The early Church always called the altar a table, *mensa*, because "altar" signifies pagan worship. The first Eucharists were held in homes, not churches. Even the technical term *eucharist* originally means meal prayer of thanksgiving. In order to recover this idea we may need to brush away the secondary symbolisms so that we can see afresh the elements which so obviously portray the Mass as a sacred meal. Christ intended that His memorial should be in the form of supper.

Centuries of Christian practice have overlaid the simple table and the food and drink with jewels of devotion arising from the varieties of theological insight mediated by the breath of the Holy Spirit. But in time this had the adverse effect of hiding that which it was intended to highlight.

Present liturgical practice must restore primary meanings so that the authentic signs authorized by Jesus may shine clearly once more.

The Mass In Parousia

A Mass loses its effectiveness if Christ is not shown forth to the world. For Christians not to carry Christ's glory into the streets of man would be a sad muffling of the very idea of Mass. Liturgists like to speak of the Mass as the anticipation of the final glory of the Savior. They look to the consumation of our age when Jesus will arrive in great glory. They quote Aquinas' *O Sacrum Convivium* to bolster the famed threefold dimension of liturgy: as a memorial of all the events in the history of salvation, the present realization of those events in a mysterious manner, and the future climax of salvation history when Christ will come glorious on the clouds of heaven and ring down the curtain of time. Much of the fire in this declaration issues from a particular view of the judgment stories in the synoptics, which revel in apocalyptic visions of Christ's triumphant second coming.

But today a different view of those texts is emerging. It notes that St. John does not speak of parousia in terms of the sky-god pictures of the synoptics, but rather of a parousia rooted in the appearances of Christ's Church. Jesus' glory shines in His Church in the final age of man. His Church becomes the light of nations, bespeaking the beauty of Christ the Savior risen from the dead and inviting all men to redemption. His angels are the Christians who in varying degrees bring the Gospel to this world, and who shine best when they manifest heartfelt love among the brethren.

Without excluding the idea of ultimate manifestation of

Christ's glory in a specialized manner, we would maintain that He has indeed already come in His Church. He is manifested by the Christian community in its evangelical and love-penetrated posture. It is the role of the Mass to help Christians be the light of the world, absorbed in the world's sin and suffering and bringing to it the healing message of Jesus and the warmth of His abiding redemptive love. A Mass without social concern for the world is hindered from being a credible Mass, for the community at the table of the Lord is meant to illumine the nations, serve the poor and share with the hateful and despairing the love of Jesus which is the center of the family of God.

Conclusion

It would be foolhardy to imagine that these seven suggestions are definitive approaches to the Eucharist, and it would be rash to conclude that they must be kept in their separateness. I have isolated each topic for purposes of clarity, hoping that the reader will undertake in thought, prayer, and lecture the harmonizing and integrating of the various parts. Many of the ideas herein have sprung from reading the new constitution on the liturgy, the works of Jean Danielou (*Bible and Liturgy, From Shadows to Reality*), and Louis Bouyer (especially, *Rite and Man*). The NCWC kit on training for the new liturgy has also been useful.

It was in a lonely spot by the sea that Jesus performed the first loaves' miracle. This was the dawn of the messianic banquet which has grown to such richness in our times. Let every catechist be faithful and true to the work of "feeding the multitudes" in our age.

Chapter 11 ❧ Teaching the Commandments

Begin with commandments in their original historical milieu. God's primary revelation of Himself in the Old Testament is as Redeemer. This is true even if Genesis begins the Bible and reveals God mainly as Creator. The creedal confession of a good Jew centered almost exclusively on God as Savior of Israel (cf. Chapter 2, "God, Our Father"). It would not be good to separate the two ideas of creation and redemption in such a way that an opposition occurs. God today continues to reveal Himself as Creator through the window of the cosmos. This is an indirect, but continuous Self-communication, whereas His Self-disclosure as Redeemer is more direct, but intermittent. The commandments come to us mainly within the context of God the Savior.

From the dawn of its history, Israel knew God in terms of redemption. God's encounter with Abraham on the plains of Haran concluded with a promise that all the nations would be blessed in the sons of the patriarch. Blessing indicates a transmission of divine life and power, one that will save them from alien spirits of evil. The story of Joseph with his huge warehouses of grain continued the sign of blessing, for here was the first clear example of other nations experiencing the blessing associated with the sons of Abraham. The plagues hurled against the house of Egypt were signs of a God of power on the threshold of one of His mightiest salvation deeds. The victory at the Reed Sea forever fixed in Jewish minds the conviction that Yahweh was their Redeemer and Lord of hosts. His demonstrations of power during the pilgrimage to Sinai were the finishing touches of the historical prologue which led up to the covenant scene and giving of the ten commandments.

The crucial text at this point is Exodus 19:3–6. God speaks to Moses: "Thus shall you say to the house of Jacob and tell the people of Israel. You have seen what I did to the Egyptians, and how I bore you on eagle's wings and brought you to myself. Now, therefore, if you will obey my voice and keep my covenant, you shall be my own possession among all the peoples, for all the earth is mine. And you shall be to me a kingdom of priests and a holy nation."

Then Moses told the people they needed to purify themselves, and restrain themselves temporarily from carnal intercourse. For three days they were to be buried, plunged into a pool of purification, sequestered from the world of the profane. "And on the morning of the third day there were thunders and lightnings and a thick cloud upon the mountain, and a very loud trumpet blast, so that all the people trembled" (Ex 19:16). The cloud glory, which was the outpouring of His Splendor, rested on Sinai. The fire symbolized the transforming power of God soon to transfigure the restless, disunited caste of runaway slaves into a people forged into unity by a common faith in Yahweh as their Savior. Their exaltation is on the third day, a common biblical image for glorification.

Moses ascends this mountain to face the glory. God gives him the ten words. The word is creative. By these ten words God creates His people. In these ten words is enshrined the heart of the Torah, the name generally given to the first five (sometimes six) books of the Bible. The root meaning of torah is "to see." Another translation is "guidance." The Torah is seeing God and the creative guiding hand of His presence.

Catechetically there is a semantic problem in teaching the Torah. We use the words "law" and "commandment," terms taken from Anglo-Saxon constitutional traditions. Un-

fortunately, these do not reflect the biblical notion of torah.
The ten words were meant to help the people perceive God's
abiding presence and guide them to self-fulfillment. They are
also meant to be seen as grateful responses to the covenant
gifts so splendidly manifest in the exodus marvels and the
pilgrimage to Sinai. The ten plagues of the Egyptian experience, classic signs of God's power, are balanced by the ten
words of Sinai, classic signs of a grateful people's acceptance
of their Lord's merciful concern. The ten words are moral
stipulations that only make sense when seen in terms of
the covenant gift. Scholars call such a covenant a suzerainty
treaty in which the king, out of personal goodness, and in
sovereign freedom, bestows vast favors on his vassal. The
vassal accepts the kingly favor and agrees to carry out certain
wishes of the king as a sign of gratitude and continued
acceptance.

All laws and commandments in Scripture and the Church,
whether moral or liturgical, must be thrust against the original
covenant insight to test their validity and to insure the spirit
in which law is to be taken. Salvation is not from the law,
either moral or cultic. Salvation is from God, and the law
is the way in which man in his freedom can accept the
salvation and retain within himself an abiding sign of that
acceptance. We do not keep the commandments in order
to be saved; we are saved first and then keep the commandments as signs of salvation and to stay saved.

The Exodus prescriptions about the ark and the tent extend
the Sinai possibilities into the realm of worship. The foundation for liturgical law is the presence of God in the ark and
tent. The shekinah-glory of God's presence is the norm that
determines what shall be done to honor Him. Blood pourings,
the book of testimony, the maintenance of sacred distance,
the symmetry, the insistence on continuity are valid as long
as they are genuine outgrowths of the original experience of
the divine presence. Hence the people of God must test
the laws composed in subsequent centuries against the cove-

nant insight at Sinai and the experience of God's presence
in the ark and the tent. If subsequent law is removed from
its original basis, then it loses life and acceptability.

Read the Book of Deuteronomy to acquire the spirit of
the moral law. Here is the religion of the book, the religion
which flows from the presence of the tablets containing the
ten words as enshrined in the ark. It is a law which declares
the immanence of God and addresses itself to the freedom
of man, urging him to surrender to a covenant Lord who
has so clearly demonstrated His love. In Deuteronomy the
ark is the shrine of testimony, that is, the monument of
Israel's faith in the declaration that God has acted in history
to make them a people. This book reminds Christians never
to forget the historical prologue to the ten words. When
commandments are studied apart from the history of salvation, then they become mere laws with no personal frame
of reference. Then commandments are only a rule book, an
impersonal code, dry and arid like the haggling of the casuists.
Speaking of the commandments without referring to God's
saving love is making them senseless, tyrannical norms. Speaking of God's saving love without ever referring to the commandments is to leave us fumbling and babbling for an
adequate response to God's love. The commandments are
a divinely inspired way of serving God and loving Him. Because our human minds could not formulate the perfect way
to serve Him, He showed us how.

Read the Book of Leviticus for a refinement of our attitude
to cultic law. Its foundation is the presence of God in the
ark and the tent. Here emphasis is on the golden mercy seat,
the strong cherubim, and the throne of Yahweh. Here is the
holy God, lofty and transcendent. The focus here is a God
who acts in perfect freedom, establishing His people in grace.
It is a picture of a Lord who takes the initiative in redemption. This is needed to balance the view of Deuteronomy
where the attention is on the response of man. It would be
foolhardy for catechesis to ignore one or the other, for God

must be perceived both in His immanence and His transcendence. Without the corrective that this balance provides, catechesis runs the danger of returning to a meaningless static liturgy on the one hand, and a cruel, enervating legalism on the other.

Read Psalm 118. Here is a song about the law. It celebrates the ten words. This psalm shows how to pray the commandments. Here is a divinely revealed contemplation of the meaning of the law. In the ascending circular thinking of the psalm one can reach the heart of the significance of the commandments. The psalm celebrates the ten words as a religious event, one which gives joy to the heart of the singer. Here it becomes clear that the commandments are not meant to make men "obligation ridden," but that freedom, joy, and peace are the true accompaniments of the commandments. So delightful is the law of the Lord that the psalmist meditates on it day and night. When God swells the heart, he runs within the freedom of the law.

Read the prophets who show that the ten words are not mere external norms, but affect the heart of man. Jeremiah in Chapter 31 speaks of a new covenant which will be written in the heart of man instead of on tablets of stone. Here he, like the other prophets, is fighting against depersonalizing the commandment. He reminds the people that the commandments are moments of personal encounter with God. The law is not just a series of propositions, but a way of meeting and loving God.

Jesus Christ came to fulfill the law. He had no intention of destroying the law. Nor did He intend to abolish the theology of the commandments which had been established by the Torah. Note how often He favorably quotes the Book of Deuteronomy. But mighty as were the deeds of God in the Exodus, the deeds of Jesus Christ, His only Son, were to be even greater. The Exodus of Jesus surpasses the Exodus of Israel. His saving act was far greater than the victory at the Reed Sea. To this newer and mightier salvation deed must be brought a newer and mightier law. This is the law of Christ.

On the new Sinai (both the mount of the beatitudes and the upper room) Jesus pronounces His new law. The theological principle was the same, namely, that the law is a response of love to the salvation deed of God. Here the horizon was more brilliant. The ten commandments were the least man could do for a loving God. Now Jesus delivers the incomparable revelation of the beatitudes and the inspiring challenge of the Sermon on the Mount. In the upper room at the Last Supper discourse, Jesus reveals His inner mind. As Isaiah and Jeremiah had provided the prophetic deepening needed to understand the ten words, so in the upper room Jesus grants a new prophetic insight, showing us the attitude we need to keep His new law. He not only gives us His law, but also the power to keep it. "With man this is impossible, but with God all things are possible." He summarized His theology of the commandments when He said, "If you love me, you will keep my commandments."

The law of Christ at the Last Supper is purposely linked to the Eucharist, because commandments must be linked to the mystery of salvation. Do not consider commandments apart from the sacraments which are the present signs of salvation. Sacraments are not just means and helps to keep the laws, but rather the reason why we must keep them. Sacraments are salvation events in which we surrender to God's love. Morality is our way of showing gratitude and acceptance of the divine initiative. St. John, who is obviously sacrament-minded, reverently places his "sermon on the mount" around the Eucharist. He has highlighted its importance by making it the last significant sermon of Jesus before His death. John did this, knowing that men will tend to love and cherish the dying words of the great and beloved.

Hence the commandments must be linked with the law of Christ to find their perfect realization. His law is an enrichment and full flowering of the original covenant. The new law is a living in Christ Jesus.

Such is the teaching of St. Paul about the law. Read his Epistle to the Romans. He shows that the old law could not save a man. It was useful as a pedagogue to Christ. The old law, of necessity, was always external to man. But the new law is written into his bones. Man now lives by the Spirit. In Chapter 8 of Romans, Paul shows that the law of Christ is an infusion of the Spirit of God into the life of man. It is by his witness and power that the details of the Sermon on the Mount and the Last Supper sermon can be kept. In the Old Testament, man still lived according to the flesh, that is, within the seemingly hopeless burden of the human condition. But now he is in the Spirit and walks by the indwelling presence of God. The new law is the salvation of man, for it is not so much a law as it is a person, with whom we have the most intimate dialogue and love. This is the dynamics of Christianity. This is what can make Paul write that the Christian is above the law. This is not an invitation to chaotic anarchy and glib exaltation of personal conscience. Paul simply assumes obedience, but understands it within the context of joyous freedom and love. It is what impels him to denounce the Pharisees of this world and offer boundless comfort to sinners. "So there is no condemnation any more for those who are in union with Christ Jesus" (Rom 8:1).

All these reflections should remind catechists of what must be the mood and framework in which they should teach the commandments. Unfortunately catechism books so situate the commandments under separate chapter headings, discuss them so abstractly that it is difficult to remember that they should be thrust against the basic covenant insight of an historical God who acted to save men. It is the duty of catechists to restore the biblical basis of law in teaching laws. Our personal experience of law can frustrate a true vision of biblical "law," hence there is need for study and readjustment of personal mentalities. As members of Western civilization and heirs to the cultural traditions of Roman law and English legal procedure we can misunderstand the real basis of biblical law which proceeds from the revelation of God in history.

It is an impoverishment of the unique approach to law which the Bible gives us to reduce it to the dimensions of human legal codes. Many of the problems of obedience and authority which plague the Church today proceed from an inadequate comprehension of the scriptural foundation of law. The perspective which revelation gives to law is one of love and personal encounter. Catechists should return to Exodus and contemplate the covenant insight, delve into Deuteronomy to see how law must be viewed in historical terms, reread the prophets for an understanding of law that rejects the impersonal. Catechists should study the transposition of the theology of law in the New Testament as it is taken over by Christ. Take advantage of the insights of form criticism into the Sermon on the Mount in which the core message is perceived and the later additions noted wherein the Christian flavor is introduced. Absorb the spirit of the Last Supper sermon for determining the inner spirit that underlies keeping the law, and its relation to the sacramental life of the Church.

Help students to overcome an abstract notion of law, in which the encounter is I-it. There is nothing very thrilling about measuring one's life against a proposition in a book. Religious orders, from which so many of our catechists come, must take their constitutions and codes of custom and bring them back to the biblical insights. How often it is said that religious must live by the Gospel of Christ, but such an evangelical posture is scarcely possible in orders which are well insulated from the prophetic words of Scripture by hundreds of small laws that seem as unchangeable as the laws of the Medes and Persians. The new catechesis presumes a new way of life for the catechist. The new theology is not meant to be a substitute formalism replacing the old one because it might be dull. These new movements in Scripture, liturgy doctrine, and catechesis are intended to change radically the Christian of today. It is an illusion to think that a mere intellectual rehashing of the new books is sufficient to be effective. Those who think this way will soon experience a frustrating chill that can demoralize them, unless they recognize the crisis as a challenge to change.

Perhaps in no other area will catechists find a greater need to change their inbred views about religion than in the area of law. The heavy-handed static tone of religious rules as well as other hardened positions of the recent past are not easily shrugged off. Patience is needed for progress, so long as patience is not a synonym for inaction. Let catechists work for change in their personal lives so that their view of law is consistent with the one they should teach and hence raise up a new generation of Christians caught by the visions of the covenants, both old and new, and enthusiastic in the exercise of their faith in freedom and the Spirit.

Chapter 12 ✤ Sin: Its Catechesis

Teachers who are familiar with the commandment-centered catechesis find few problems in explaining the nature of sin and how one is committed. Each commandment is confidently held up to the student's gaze, and pupil is given a glimpse of the variety of ways in which the command can be broken. Lists of sins have been common in the Church ever since the days of St. Paul. But is this enough? Does this cool enumeration of sins flash lights in the minds of students, jolting them to avoid sin because they have come to an awareness of its personal nature? Can an abstract, impersonal theology of sin awaken young minds to its real meaning, fill them with a calm and firm desire never to sin?

I would urge teachers to return to the Bible to correct the unbalanced catechesis of sin that has been prevalent. The Bible avoids the pitfalls of the monster and the angel, admitting, indeed, that sin is monstrous, but balancing its views with the mercy of God. In the following paragraphs I will outline the biblical theme of sin, in the hope that the dynamic correctives of Scripture will restore to catechesis a style and validity often missing in present teaching.

*   *   *

Cardinal Newman once wrote, "You cannot write sinless literature about a sinful people." Biblical literature has never feared to portray the sinfulness of man, whether the man be a saintly prophet or king, or a hateful tyrant. It looks as uncompromisingly on the sin of David as on the aberrations of Jezebel. Rather than declare what man thinks of sin, the

Bible unerringly announces what God teaches about sin. Men come to know the real meaning of sin by hearing the word of the Lord and confronting His actions in history.

Sin events are *personal* matters in the Bible. God patrols the garden of Eden, calling for Adam, demanding a confrontation. God views the bloodstained earth and summons Cain to the bar of judgment. The prophet Nathan thrusts his finger into the face of David, and accuses the king of murder and adultery. God reminds our first parents that their sin was eating from His special tree; He nags Cain with the assertion that the blood cries out to Him for vengeance; and in the parable of Nathan God scolds David for having killed the lamb which He loved so much.

The sin situation of Scripture is a cyclical matter. Sin is not considered abstractly or alone, but in relation to what precedes it and what consequences ensue. The Book of Judges expresses the cyclical style as well as any text of the Bible. "And the people of Israel did what was evil in the sight of the Lord, and served the Baals. . . . So the anger of the Lord was kindled against Israel, and he sold them into the power of their enemies. Then the people of the Lord cried to God, and he raised up judges who saved them from the power of those that plundered them" (Jgs 2:11–16; cf. 3:7–9; 4:1–3; 6:1–11). The biblical writers intend to portray sin against the broader background than the sin itself in order to retain the corrective of redemption. The rhythm is one of sin, punishment, penance, and salvation, a dialogic structure in which there is a give-and-take between God and the people.

This is why sin narratives often conclude with redemption symbols, events, or savior figures. The sin of Adam bows before the seed of the promise; Cain's hopelessness is tempered by the reassuring mark God put on his forehead. The stormy waters of the deluge, ruthlessly washing away the sins of this world, simmer calmly in the colors of the covenant rainbow. Exodus and Calvary-Resurrection are the climactic salvation moments of all history. Samson, David, and Isaiah are but three of a multitude of savior figures of sacred history. The sin-grace dialectic is so common in the pages of the Bible that it is astonishing in afterthought to see how catechesis could ever have been reduced to a theological negativism, scaring people with the fires of hell without the rainbowed horizons of redemption.

The sin events of Scripture go hand in hand with theological reflection. The paschal sermons of Deuteronomy are a prophetic interpretation of Israel's desert experience in which the memorable story of the golden calf emerges as the archetype of Israel's sinfulness, and God's wrathful hand is always steady enough to keep Him from repeating the deluge catastrophe, because at least He will be faithful to the covenant promise to lead Israel into the Holy Land. He evokes the darkness of faith as He speaks out of the fire and cloud, heard, but not seen. He evokes the brightness of love by raising up luminous figures such as Moses and Joshua and the judges, whose transparency communicates some glimpse of divinity.

As Deuteronomy lights up the landscape of the Exodus, the prophets clarify the meaning of the monarchy and the exile. The prophets assume the role of theologians of history, unafraid to declare that the downfall of the monarchy is a direct result of the sins of Israel. The Deuteronomic theologian concentrates on the collective personality of the people, stating that their sin is a refusal to accept the salvation wrought in the Exodus, a rejection symbolized by their steady infidelity to the covenant. Prophetic theologians shift the emphasis from the collective level to the individual personal level, inferring that sin lies in the heart of men who operate from a vantage point of responsibility and freedom. An individual's sin affects the destiny of the nation, but it also can foresee a specialized retribution.

St. Paul continues the prophetic style of reflection upon the history of God's dealing with His people, this time in

His Son, Jesus. Paul provides us with vivid lines about the kingdom of "the principalities and the powers," who rule the darksome realm of this world. He relates the idea of sin to the daily struggle against the kingdom of evil. He lists catalogues of sins in several of his epistles, sometimes ending with an admonition that those who so act cannot enter the kingdom of heaven. His teaching about faith, justification, and baptism includes his major insights into the meaning of sin.

The biblical theme of sins begins with the first eleven chapters of Genesis, which I would term the Adam cycle, including the Cain murder tale, the savagery of Lamech, and the story of Noah and the deluge. The sacred author is not trying to answer the question why sin entered the world, but stating the well-known fact that sin inhabits the earth. By using Mesopotamian folktales he weaves a poem describing sin and its effects and, above all, the greatness of God who will overcome sin. He uses the misery of sin and the human conditions as a black panel to illustrate the shining mercy of God. All biblical sin stories begin with man experiencing some gesture of God's love. Eden is the archetype of God's initial posture toward man. The refusal of Eden is the archetype of man's regrettable reaction to God's personal love, rejecting it in preference to some self-appointed center of existence.

Sin breaks the personal relation between God and man. The fearful couple hide in the bushes, already exiling themselves before God utters the decree of expulsion. Sin also separates men from each other, as the story of Cain and the savage chant of Lamech indicate: "I have slain a man for wounding me, a young man for striking me. If Cain is avenged sevenfold, truly Lamech seventy-sevenfold" (Gn 4: 23–24). Finally sin corrupts the very earth itself. "Now the earth was corrupt in God's sight, and the earth was filled with violence. And God saw the earth, and behold it was corrupt, for all the flesh had corrupted their way upon the earth" (Gn 8:11–12). Sin, then, is social and cosmic as well as being an individual affair. Once God's love is rejected, men destroy their relationships with Him with each other and with the world. Sin is divisive, projecting men into a hopeless loneliness, characterized by the anguished cry of Cain: "My punishment is greater than I can bear. Behold, you have driven me this day away from the ground; and from your face I shall be hidden; and I shall be a fugitive and a wanderer upon the earth, and whoever finds me shall slay me" (Gn 4:13–14). God's ultimate weapon is the deluge which washes away the sins of the earth. But the dialectic of redemption abides in the seed promised to Adam, the protective mark on the forehead of Cain and the survival of the just man and savior figure, Noah.

Much as God works to restore man, sin has a nagging way of staying around. As out of the chaos of Genesis 1, God brought forth the life of the earth, so out of the deluge chaos God summons forth a new creation from the ark, symbol of the Church. From the ark come two of every kind of animal, and the just man, Noah, and his family. In time, these too will break their relationship with Him through sin, but now the writer shifts our attention to the rainbow in the sky that spans the whole length of the earth, with its reassuring message, that no matter how sinful man becomes, God has established a covenant with the cosmos, and will somehow rescue man from the ultimate catastrophe of the human condition of separateness from Him, from fellowmen, and from the land.

The original sin of mankind repeats itself in the original sin of Israel. Israel is led by God into the Eden of the desert. There God treats her like a bride with flashing fountains of water, bread from heaven, and meat from the winds. The great wedding day is at Sinai, where God grants His covenant. Ironically it was at the very moment when God was concluding this covenant that the people demanded of Aaron, "Make us a God to march before us" (Ex 32:1). Ezekiel describes this vividly: "You took off your garments and made yourselves gaily decked shrines. You took your splendid ornament of gold and silver, which I had given you, and made for yourselves images of men with which you played the harlot. My oil and my incense you placed before them" (Ez 16: 16–19).

As Adam refused God's love symbolized by the garden of Eden, Israel refused His love typified by the Exodus redemption and the gifts of the desert. As the Adam cycle fatally descended into the chaos of the deluge, so the Israel cycle descends into the chaos of the exile. The story of the judges illustrates the problem of idolatry. The history of the monarchy demonstrates the progressive secularism of Israel amid tales of murder, civil war, internal strife, adultery, and diplomatic intrigue, ending in the fall of the monarchy, the slaughter of the people, the burning of their cities, and the enslavement of the remnant in the Babylonian exile. Separateness is once again the result of sin — Israel running to the temple prostitute at the Canaanite shrine of Gaza. Civil war separates the northern tribes from the south, brother fighting against brother as in the case of Cain and Abel. Samaria and Judah form alliances with the mighty powers of the earth, as did the daughters of men wed the giants of the land (cf. Gn 6:1–4).

Still God keeps alive the dialectic of redemption. Great savior figures crowd the pages of Israel's history. Moses, Joshua, Deborah, Samuel, David, Ezekiel, Josiah, Isaiah, and many others perpetually resurrect the ideal of covenant salvation from sin. Barak's victory on the plains of Esdraelon, the ark's journey to Jerusalem, the dedication of the temple, the reform of King Josiah are salvation moments that raise the people from their apostate ways. Even in the dark waters of the exile, the holy remnant, like the ark of old, sustains the hope that God will be faithful to the earth. The stirring sermons of second Isaiah announce a new Exodus (Chap. 40) and a covenant that will be everlasting:

Arise, shine, for your light has come,
    And the glory of the Lord has risen upon you.
And nations shall come to your light,
    And kings to the brightness of your rising.
The sun shall be no more
    Your light by day,
Nor, for brightness shall the moon
    Give light to you by night,
But the Lord will be your everlasting light
    And your God will be your glory.

[Read all of Isaiah 60]

The whiplash of the prophetic condemnation of sin is a human image of the divine anger against sin, and, salutary as it may be, it should not obscure the efforts of the prophets to relate sin to human responsibility. Prophets declare that sin is a personal matter, and human beings must take the responsibility for it. Jeremiah, in his temple sermon (cf. Chap. 7), criticizes the worshipers for muttering pious phrases in magical fashion, hoping that the incantation shall wipe away their sins, even though they have no intention of changing their hearts and entering into a true personal relationship with God once more.

Isaiah has a classical sermon against Israelites who love liturgical ceremonies and feasts, but who never really meet God, because they are attached to sins that maintain them in separateness from Him. "What is the multitude of your sacrifices to me? I have had enough of burnt offerings of rams. I do not delight in the blood of bulls. Who requires of you this trampling of my courts? Bring no more vain offerings; incense is an abomination to me. Your new moons and appointed feasts *my soul hates!*" Of course God is not against liturgy, for He certainly wants a reverent and loyal worship from His people that they may acknowledge Him as Lord of all, enter into communion with Him, and expiate their sins. Here He is condemning the hypocrisy of worshiping when the people are attached to sin, and hence separated from Him. "Your hands are full of blood. Wash yourselves clean. Seek justice, correct oppression, defend the fatherless, plead for the widow." (Read all of Isaiah 1.)

In the dark ages of the postexilic period, Israel became a community of faith, withdrawing from the broil of history's vacillations to contemplate the state of man and to see deeper into the sin situation. These mystical members of the wisdom movement began to describe the subjective states of sinful man, to wrestle with the problems of evil. The tortured Job, the suffering just man as the Psalms and of Isaiah 53, are profound biblical attempts to face the effects of sin in the anguished heart of man.

The Old Testament shows that the love of God precedes and succeeds all sin events. The privileges of Eden are a prelude to the original sin of Adam, but the darkness of the fall is relieved by the rainbow heralding the cosmic covenant. The dramatic gesture of divine love at the exodus, implemented by the gifts of the desert during the pilgrimage to Sinai, is scarred by the original sin of Israel at the shrine of the golden calf. But God is faithful and forgiving, establishing the mosaic covenant. The theme of the golden calf carried through judges and the sad days of the monarchy gives way to the joyous gospel of Isaiah in which God Himself will be the light of His people.

The Old Testament God is not, then, an angry God, nor is the story a dialogue of sin and anger. The Old Testament testimony situates sin against a background of God's love tirelessly shown. Sin is a refusal to remain in the tension of relation with God, an action characterized by the failure to accept His love. Prophetic personalism and the introspective mysticism of the wisdom writers round out the general impression left by the old covenant.

*   *   *

The saving deeds and words of Jesus continue the disclosure of the divine attitude about sin. The major saving deeds of Jesus are His miracles and these partake of the same quality which the mighty deeds of His Father possessed in the Old Testament. They are a frontal attack on sin and evil. The God of Moses rained down plagues to throw back the forces of pharaoh. Now Jesus thrusts His mighty wonders against the forces of evil in Galilee and Judah, driving out demons, purifying men from sin, bringing mercy and peace to repentant harlots. His healings, resurrections, and cosmic deeds stood as signs of the arrival of the kingdom of God on earth, the longed-for Day of the Lord, so much stressed by the prophets of the golden age. The evil spirits prevent men from having a love relationship with God, hence they must be expelled.

Jesus, the innocent Lamb, transforms Galilee into a new Eden. But as both Adam and Israel rebelled, so now the hostility appears and His loving gestures are misunderstood and rejected. The time of enchantment is over, and once again man refuses the work of God. Christ's first reaction is to reduce the number of His signs, withdraw from public life, and concentrate on forming a holy remnant which will be the seed of His new Church. His miracles, which were signs of the conquest of sin, now are seen as symbols of contradiction, confusing many, and polarizing men into attitudes of acceptance and rejection. Jesus assumes the mantle of the prophets, curses the fig tree, drives the traders from the temple, and pronounces judgment on Jerusalem.

The existence of sin has always brought men eventually to ponder the problem of evil. Israel's earliest experience with God indicated that if they were faithful to the covenant, they would be blessed. Blessing meant large families, rich harvests, and the perpetuation of the ancestral name. But in time they noticed that sometimes the just man suffered. The Book of Job is a parable about a just man who suffered terribly, and whose solution was summed up in the famed recital of faith: "The Lord gives; the Lord takes away. Blessed be the name of the Lord." But Isaiah carried the argument a step further. When the just man suffers, he does a work of

God, by assuming into the fires of his pain the sins of the world, going into the pit of destruction, there to await the resurrection only God could give. The sacrifices of animals could not properly solve the problem of evil, for an animal could not consciously take on the sins of the world. Further the suffering servant of Isaiah (Chap. 53) was emblematic of some great and mysterious atonement figure who would come on the day of the Lord and assume the sins of all.

Jesus is the long-awaited Suffering Servant who makes an Easter journey through the dark waters of death as a perfect expiation deed for the guilt of men and as a glorious offering of Self to the Father. This journey was a march to glory and the definitive victory over sin. The Last Supper is established as an enduring memorial of the perfect salvation act and a covenant action by which all future generations can identify with the journey of Christ. Calvary is the sign whereby sin is condemned. Resurrection is the sign of the victory over sin. The outpouring of the Spirit is the sign of the Church, which is a community that witnesses that the human condition need no longer cruelly dominate men. Every Christian has been incorporated into the paschal journey of Christ through death to victory over sin by the sacrament of baptism. But what has been accomplished sacramentally must now be spelled out existentially. Christian existence is the living sign that redemption can be accepted and that the loneliness and separateness of sin need not be the norm of human life. Christian existence is the hallelujah shout thrust against all the phony philosophies of men, and the iron anvils of dictators, and the vague stoicism of intellectuals. Christian existence frowns on those who end it all by applying razor blades to their wrists, challenging this as cowardly, and summoning men to assume the cross of existence itself that the noble life of resurrection may be theirs.

With all the above in mind I believe that catechists should come to see that their primary concern is sin before sins. So many times catechesis bogs down in a discussion of

whether or not a given action is a sin, whereas the fundamental question is, "What is sin?" I am well aware that
the psalmist asks, "Who can understand sin?" This is a
proper question because it attends to the fact that sin is a
mystery, just as much as grace is. Sin does not seem so
mysterious if we are simply looking at what is generally
considered a bad act. But sin can be evaluated as a mystery
when viewed as a break in a person's relation with God,
fellowman, and the cosmos. A true grasp of the meaning
of sin grows in proportion to our understanding of the meaning of relations between persons. The covenants of the Bible
are I-Thou relationships. Because the ego of God is involved,
naturally we can never probe the mystery perfectly, but even
in the order of human relations there is a uniqueness that
no observer will ever fully comprehend. Furthermore, sin
must be seen against the background of a relationship in
which Christ is a Redeemer who wants His beloved to walk
the way of the cross, be dedicated to death, in order to know
the glory of resurrection. True, we do not walk alone, for
God leads us in Christ by the power of His Holy Spirit.
The arena for this journey is the sacramental life, the community of the Church, and the myriad of human relations
each of us daily encounter. Once relation is on the way to
mastery then let casuistry be admitted. Then let conversation abound about "sins," for it is obvious that concrete
situations will reveal the quality of our relation to God, and
hence need discussion, clarification, and determination.

The Apocalypse tells of the final state of sin. The last trumpets sound a frightful blast after an eerie half hour of silence
in heaven. Then, amid piercing sounds of trumpets, fire mixed
with blood, falling stars, and darkened suns, evil perishes from
the earth. After this is heard the triumphant song of redemption: "Praise the Lord. . . . Let us be glad and triumphant, and
give him glory, for the marriage of the lamb has come. . . .
Blessed are they who are invited to the marriage supper of the
lamb!" (Ap 19:7–9.)

Chapter 13 ✱ Biblical Symbol and Intuitive Relevance*

Relevancy is a battle cry of the modern Church. But it is not often certain what relevancy is. There are as many relevancies as there are people, it seems. I wish to treat of relevancy and the Bible, and for this I will need to make a relationship with symbol. I shall begin with a coverage of my own view of relevancy and then proceed to make a link with biblical symbol.

The most obvious form of relevancy is that which deals with action. A dynamic society such as ours is quick to burn incense before plans of activism, opting for solid practical results. Its proponents think a great deal of what the Church ought to be doing in the modern world, and it has spawned a corps of enthusiastic Christians whose lives are pictures of involvement with social concerns such as civil rights, world poverty, and birth control. Ethical relevance will always be popular in a moral universe, and rightly so.

A second form of relevance is intellectual concern. How does the Christian message body itself forth against the stimulating intellectual challenges of today? As anthropology with nagging insistence moves toward intimations of polygenism, what will Adam and Eve do? As Teilhard de Chardin presents us with the sacrament of evolution and his theories of prelife, what shall be the response of established dogma and the hardened intellectual postures of the past? As Marxism accuses Christianity's God of being unreal, whence will arise the capacity of self-reflection and honest examination to test

---

* Reprinted by arrangement with *The Bible Today*.

the truth or falsehood of these challenges? There is a special area of relevancy for the intellectual as well as for the social crusader.

Further there is such a thing as intuitive relevance. By this I mean touching man at a point of deepest emotion. I discount surface emotional responses here, reactions such as trembling or giggling, sweaty palms or overt sexual drive. I am rather affirming an almost intangible shock similar to the tremors felt on the surface of the earth, produced by some nameless loosening of the foundation in the dark below, but scarcely visible on the landscape. Intuitive relevance occurs when a man is deeply moved, an involuntary stillness that momentarily shuts off external response. This can be produced by a shock of beauty as manifested in poetry, music, literary symbol, or archetypal action.

Last, there is ontological relevance. Here I mean a shaping of attitudes. This would be an invisible surgery and molding of disposition. It is preethical and so determinant of moral procedure. Such a sculpturing of inner drives is an imperative form of relevance and easily disposed of by the fast buck, computerized modern man. Even the new Church will need to pause in the tumultuous wake of newly discovered freedoms, picket lines, and starry-eyed idealists, and wonder about the shaping of attitudes. I think that the inevitable consolidation that will follow the Council will include a thoughtful concern for this sort of relevance. The coming generation in the Church is young, with all the glory and wastefulness of youth, and the lack of temper that only time can bring.

Intellectual and ethical relevance are direct forms, while intuitive and ontological relevance are indirect. I feel that the indirect is superior to the direct, and ought always to be the prize despite its elusiveness. The mysterious event of intuitive relevance lies at the root of all successful endeavor. It charges the fire of attitude reform, and saves the mind from intellectualism and the ethical drive from moralism.

I do not pretend that this is easy to come by, and I would not cheapen it by wishing it to be so.

Since I think intuitive relevance is all important then I must state how it is touched. I think the principal instrument is the symbol, especially the symbol of Scripture. By symbol, I mean an image that bears a message, both natural and theological. The image may be a picture, a poem, a piece of music or a story that has historical-mythical content. The image speaks for itself, but it also speaks for a presence that is not so evident. The images of Scripture are such, speaking their own meaning, and proclaiming a presence not always easily discernible. In calling a biblical story a symbol, I do not enter into the controversy about historicity, because there is not a necessary contradiction between symbol and history.

To many Americans, symbol is a bad word. Our fact-finding people feel uneasy about discussions of symbol because it seems a repudiation of the real. This is the result of hurry, which is intolerant both of symbol and the ambiguity which is its necessary counterpart. Symbol demands a stop sign and the power to look without the pressure of reflection. At the moment our speed-up society does not have the time.

As to the symbols of the Bible, here are some solutions to approaching them. First, scratch the symbol, but save the message. Rudolf Bultmann has led this parade for a long time with his pack of demythologizers. It would be patronizing in the extreme to cipher his work because I do not share his view of the biblical myth, for he has made a singular contribution to all Christians by his restoration of the existential challenge of the biblical message. But his clean severance of the message from the symbol implies that the symbol speaks no language of its own, and that conceptualizing is the only way to divine truth.

A second approach to symbol is to retain the symbol and message intact and throw it stonelike against the Christian. This is the method of Karl Barth who in extraordinary obedi-

ence to the Word and dauntless confidence in its power
bodies the symbol unshaven in any manner or form against
his congregation. But in so doing he ignores the very problem that led Bultmann to abandon the symbol, namely,
that modern intolerance with symbol caused by haste and
the empirical mind. It is like a rubber ball bobbing across
the slippery hands of boys in a swimming pool.

A third avenue to the biblical symbol is to save the message and design new symbols that have more immediate appeal for the modern mind. Instead of the archetypal myth
of the flood, retell the story in terms of the bomb at Hiro-
shima. The language analysts are prominent in this field, going so far as to publish a book entitled *The Secular Gospel
of Jesus*. I think these efforts are good and necessary but I do
not think they are the solution.

Hence the fourth suggestion. Save the old biblical symbols and their message, but resituate them. This means that
we should remove from them whatever debris hides them
from shining today. It is not right to teach the natural speaking of a symbol, though it is imperative to teach its theological meaning. Teaching the symbolism of a candle makes little
sense if the candle is never allowed to speak for itself. A
candle is speechless in a room flooded with thousands of
watts of electricity. But situate it by removing the light and
bringing in darkness and then the candle will utter its natural
message. Only then does the theological rubric intrude as
Christ's words, "I am the light of the world," are linked to it.

The monumental scientific contributions to the Bible from
the study rooms of the philologists, the pick and shovel of
the archaeologists, and the jigsaw puzzle tables of the Dead
Sea scrollery are not meant to hide the biblical symbols but
rather to peel away the cultural shells that obscure them.
In reading the story of the ordeal of Isaac, scientific studies
set the tone of the event and remind us that in this particular story, the main thing to remove is haste. It is a tale

that demands an unhurried and involved seeing of the event that takes place. I do not mean seeing in the sense of an Ignatian meditation, but simply a looking. The theme is one of anguish, and anguish takes place.

Situating a symbol is a *via negativa*, stripping away that which blinds us. Perhaps hearing is a better image than seeing when discussing the scriptural symbol. To appreciate classical music we shut out from our range of hearing all that interferes with hearing the work, and our love grows through much replaying of the record. Similarly the biblical symbol is meant to be heard. There are levels of hearing, of course. Listening to the chatter at a cocktail party is not the same as listening to the words of the beloved. The biblical symbol must be heard in such a way that a resonance is established in the inner man. Personal bias and prejudice can be silenced by the scholarly apparatus of scientific Scripture studies, provided we have escaped the pitfall of total fascination with the Nuzu tablets to the exclusion of the illumination which they give to the Genesis narratives. Scientism is a temptation in Scripture too.

Now to return to my original remarks about intuitive relevance. In all relevance we are dealing with the challenge and response. In this case the challenge shouts from the sacred page through symbol, laden with archetypal and theological power. It demands an intuitive response, in that it brings the surrendering believer to a deeply moving religious experience, from which should flow a gradual reshaping of his attitudes. It is a shaking of the foundations. And as the tremors die away, the intellect begins its process of reflection, bending back on the event, and eventually gives direction to ethical output.

Father Davis, in his book *Theology for Today*, speaks much about the danger of irrelevancy, and the principal targets of his remarks are the new Scripture men and their followers, who, he implies, can be caught up in this fascinating revolu-

tion in a way that they produce a new formalism to replace
the old and a new irrelevancy as a substitute for the old.
These reflections on the role of biblical symbol and intuitive
relevance are designed to help avoid the danger cited by
Father Davis and to excite some thinking and perhaps controversy about this subject.

Chapter 14 ❦ Witness:

Your Prophetic Stance in the Church

As always we must research the biblical perspective of witness. We must know what God has said long before we worry about what man has said about prophetic witness. To find out what prophecy should be you must look at the prophets. What are the prophets like and what have they done? In scanning the prophets I noticed that one of their continuing major experiences is to "see the heavens opened." Ezekiel looks up to heaven and sees it open (cf. Ezek 1:1). What did he see? He sees flying saucers, burning suns, and disks. Standing by the River Chobar in prosperous Babylon he views the world-famous hanging gardens in patterns of red and gold. He sees the great wall of the city, a hundred feet high, and so wide at the top it could support a chariot race.

Other prophets have seen the heavens opened also. Moses in the twenty-fourth chapter of the Exodus is taking a walk with his sister, Miriam, after the great covenant scene. Here Moses sees God walking on a sapphire pavement. It is in the afterglow of the covenant that the greatest of the prophets sees God. The vision is a way of saying that God comes to man in the context of the alliance. Why is there an alliance in the first place? Because God does not want to be too distant from us and we want Him close to us, so that we can have life through continuous contact with Him. Moses sees the heavens opened when his covenant experience is confirmed.

Isaiah, too, on the threshold of his vocation, sees the heavens opened. Chapter 6 of Isaiah describes the prophet attending a liturgical service at which he perceives, through the thick darkness of the holy of holies, God appearing to him, not in the symbols of worship, but in the reality of his own presence. He heard a song when the heavens opened, that tells him that the earth and the heavens are filled with the glory of God. This enabled Isaiah to see the divine presence from that day forward in the heart of the cosmos. The radiance of God's glory is perceptible to Isaiah. This is what he sees when the heavens are opened.

Jesus, also, sees the heavens opened. As a true prophet He sees heaven opened. All the Gospels tell the story of His baptism in the Jordan, when Jesus is initiated into His prophetic career. What does He see? His Father. What does He hear? The Father says, "You are my son, in whom I am well pleased." This text is a taping together of Psalm 2 ("You are my Son") and the servant poem of Isaiah 42. It means that Jesus is a royal Davidic son who shall be Messiah, and a Redeemer who must suffer. Catechists who exercise a prophetic role should meditate on the first servant poem of Isaiah to learn some of the qualities of a prophet. God is pleased with real prophets, and puts His Spirit upon them. This is done even to Jesus, as a sort of messianic investiture, similar to the vesting and clothing ceremonies of religious. The Spirit is poured out that the prophet might "bring justice to the nations," that is, bring salvation to the world. The religious habit is a symbol of prophecy, a witness garment. The Jordan vision tells all prophets that God loves them, and that they have a mission. They are not to stand still, but go forth and save the world.

Stephen looked up into heaven and saw Jesus standing in glory. It is the privilege of all Christians to know, as did Stephen, not the historical Jesus of Galilee, but the post-ascended Christ, the Lord of glory. If this Stephen-oriented vision is not operative in catechists, it is quite possible that a wrong view of Christ can be taught. To look only at the preascended or preresurrected Christ is unreal, for the only Christ who exists now is the risen Lord. Have you ever noticed how little Paul speaks of the Christ of Galilee and Jerusalem. Contrast his view with the Gospel picture. He preached before the Gospel was written, and tells no stories about Christ. For him the major insight was to know and declare Jesus dead and risen, for in this is the substance of the mystery of Christ. Stephen saw this and became a witness — in the greatest sense of that term, martyr. When martyrs became less fashionable, men found new ways to witness, namely, in the founding of the religious orders.

Paul looked up to heaven on the Damascus road. What did he see? The Church. Prophets must look up to heaven and see the new Jerusalem. In the Apocalypse the prophet sees the new Jerusalem descending from heaven down to earth. Catechists must be absorbed with a vision of the Church, especially today when so much new work has been done to help us understand the Church. The principal theological question of our age is "What is the Church?" The Second Vatican Council struggled several years to establish guidelines for fresh answers. Its Constitution on the Church and the articles in the journals are the present source from which catechists can read about the new thinking on the mystery of the Church. A real prophet today will work hard to realize what is the meaning of the Church, especially as it exists in the world today. Paul was struck from his horse when he saw the Church. Let catechists today be willing to be shaken up a little, so they can look up into heaven and see the "new Church."

Peter looked up into heaven at the transfiguration. He remembered well that experience, made a note of it, and later on from a prison cell recorded it in Second Peter 1:16–21. "For we did not follow cleverly devised myths when we made known to you the power and the coming of our Lord Jesus Christ, but we were eyewitnesses of his majesty." A catechist should teach in this spirit, confident of being an eyewitness of the majesty of Jesus. Jesus is still present in the world, through the biblical word, through the Eucharist, but above all through the people of God, the Church. It is the people of God who are the majesty of Jesus in this world. John says that the Church, when it loves credibly, is the parousia of Christ in glory. Of course it must be a credible Church, that is, one in which the perfect teaching of Christ is boldly and unashamedly proclaimed. A Church that refuses to announce the full message of Jesus is an incredible Church and there is no majesty in it; hence its members cannot be eyewitnesses. Our Church must be believable. It is not enough to be a member of a religious order, you must appear and act in such a way that the order's ideals are clear. Peter's witness then is to see the majesty of the Church. Today's prophets must work for a credible Church so that this majesty will not be veiled.

John the presbyter, author of the Apocalypse, saw the heavens opened. He saw a white horse, whose rider wore a cloak splattered in blood and on whose thigh was written the word of God. Good prophets see God's word when they look to heaven. Good prophetical catechists hear the word of the Lord. God spoke a long time ago and His voice was quiet when He said, "Let there be light." Through history His voice grew louder as He said: "Let there be earth, men, Abraham, Moses and Jesus and Church." The rider on the white horse must stride through the world making heard the voice of the Lord. This rider is the catechist, obedient to the word and faithful to its ministry.

Prophets see the heavens opened, though their feet are squarely on the earth. Their basic orientation is toward God, deriving their message from His word, not just from a textbook. They do not take their message mainly from theology books or treatises on mysticism. The mystic may seem to float above reality, while the theologian can seem to be having a dialogue with himself. The word of God is a record of a dialogue between the prophet and his Lord.

Good prophets must eat the scroll. When Jeremiah was appointed a prophet, God came to him and handed him a scroll, and said, "Jeremiah, I want you to be my prophet." The prophet replied that this was impossible, "I am not a very good speaker." God remembered that Moses made the same objection, claiming to be a stutterer. But God said to Jeremiah, "Don't complain to me that you are but a babbler like a child. You will be my prophet." Jeremiah agreed, "I'll take scroll home and study it." "No you won't," said God, "I want you to eat it right here." Recall at this point the Introit for the Mass of a Confessor: "The mouth of the just man shall meditate wisdom." Meditate is a polite English word here for "chew." It is eating the word of God, absorbing it until it becomes bone of your bone, like oil that is rubbed into muscle. Prophets must not just know the Bible, but feel the Scripture. Presenting the word to others must be done in such a way that it seems true, that it is felt as fact. Recapture the sagalike quality of Scripture in which the author recalls the event in the glow of the wonder in which it was experienced. This is eating the scroll.

Prophets must experience the burning coal. When Isaiah, all unwittingly, was introduced into the divine glory, and heard the angels sing, he was absorbed by the beauty and greatness of the scene. When, however, the smoke screen hid the vision from him, he stood back all alone with his thoughts. He peered into the dark confessional of his soul, conducting an examination of conscience, seeing himself over against the divine glory. How did he compare? He saw that he was a sinner. "Woe is me, I am a man of unclean lips" (Is 6:4). This is what every prophet must do, namely, begin with the fact that he is a sinner.

Sin is still abroad in this world, and no catechist is totally free from the threat of its power and influence. How many catechists read spiritual books, study about humility, but note little about sin? How many spiritual books really treat the reality of sin? Many of the treatises that find their way into convents and monasteries seem to minister to a brand of human being who somehow no longer knows the presence or the power of sin. This is an illusion.

Any honest observer knows that no religious community is made up of angels, but rather of men and women in whose hearts remains the sting of alienation with which the human condition is familiar and the death dread which is sin's wages. But prophets need not be discouraged, because God has a burning coal of baptism, confirmation, and the Eucharist to purify and save us. When His burning coal touches us we are made clean. The biblical image of transformation is fire. Malachi (3:1–5) elaborates on this theme of purification of the prophet: "Behold, I send my messenger before me, and the Lord whom you seek will suddenly come to his temple. But who can endure the day of his coming and who can stand when he appears. For he is like a refiner's fire and like a fuller's soap. He will sit as a refiner and purifier of silver, and he will purify the sons of Levi and refine them like gold and silver, till they present right offerings to the Lord."

A real prophet challenges his audience. Prophets are not afraid. Prophets have a way of making people feel uneasy. They are raised up by God to change their generation. Such a man was Teilhard de Chardin. His thinking will change a generation. Yet he has raised and continues to raise controversial emotions. He was stoned and rejected by the people of his own age. Typical prophets are often persecuted by the men of their own time. Prophets challenge their contemporaries to change. This is an uncomfortable exhortation, because it is a threat to security.

Jeremiah was afraid at first, but God told him not to fear for He would remain with him. "The Lord stretched forth his hand and touched my mouth. 'See, I have set you today over nations and kingdoms, to pluck up and break down, to destroy and overthrow, to build and to plant'" (Jer 1:10). Here is no sweet catechesis, or saccharine religion. No prophet may destroy a person's faith in himself, unless he is also prepared to rebuild the person into a better Christian. Catechesis is not a totally negative work; it is also positive. Prophets must not fear, for God is their mighty fortress. "I make you this day a fortified city, an iron pillar, and a bronze wall. Enemies will fight against you, but they shall not prevail, for I am with you, says the Lord" (Jer 1:18–19).

Jeremiah did lose his fear and spoke in fury to the people of his age. "Be appalled, Oh heavens at this; be shocked. For my people have forsaken the fountains of living waters and hewed out sewers for themselves. . . . Though you wash yourself with lye and use much soap, the stain of your guilt is still before me. Why do you say to a tree: 'You are my father'; or to a stone, 'You gave me birth' " (Jer 2:12–13, 22, 27). But in his thirty-first chapter he balances the picture off with signs of mercy, offering comfort to Rachel, the symbol of national tragedy, and announcing the advent of a new covenant.

The prophet must suffer for he is a witness of the cross. The Gospel is a word of the cross. The fifty-third chapter of Isaiah vividly describes the need of the prophet to suffer. Sometimes the suffering is beyond belief. "Who could have believed our report? The most beautiful of the sons of men is beaten, and all we, like sheep, have gone stray, and he has borne the burden of us all" (Is 53:1, 4, 6). Prophets must suffer for their cause.

The confessions of Jeremiah are filled with references to the anguish of prophecy. He never wanted to be a preacher. He was a small-town boy, from Anatoth, and the son of a local priest. His grandfather had been a priest as well. So it was natural that he should enter the priesthood. But the unexpected occurred. God, in the vocation vision, thrust this sensitive young man up to the big city. He must witness in Jerusalem, heart of the nation, scene of intrigue, and the undercurrent battle of power between temple officials and the palace guard. Jeremiah disliked his job. He feared criticism and hated opposition. He certainly was not thick-skinned.

After one of his sermons the city officials were so angry that they sentenced him to a night in the stocks. All night the wind blew against him and the dampness fell upon him. Passersby gave him a kick and spit on him. Here is what he wrote about it. "I have become a laughing stock all the day; everyone mocks me. Whenever I speak, I cry out: violence and destruction. For the word of the Lord has become for me a reproach and derision all day long. If I say, 'I won't preach any more in God's name,' there is in my heart a burning fire, shut up in my bones, and I'm tired of holding it in" (Jer 20:7–9). Yet he cheers up fast: "Sing to the Lord; praise the Lord, for he has delivered the life of the needy from the hand of the evil doers" (Jer 20:13).

Catechists will have to suffer, for the errors of past catechesis, for a Church that did not remember its mission to the world. This is not casting an accusing finger at the past, for no one doubts the energy and sincerity of our fathers. Our insight is a unique gift of this age and we can take no credit for it.

Finally, prophets are witnesses of redemption. Much as the prophets rage against sin, they are equally enthusiastic in describing the day of the Lord when salvation will triumph. Ezekiel abounds with fresh and appealing redemptive instruction. After a fierce crack at irresponsible shepherds (Chap. 34), his word for Israel's leaders, he movingly describes God as the good shepherd who saves His people — a promise realized perfectly in Christ. After a sermon on regeneration, he recounts the strange vision in the field of dry bones (Chaps. 36–37) regenerated by the salvation breath of God's Spirit. The glory of God had left the temple because of the people's sins. Now this glory returns as an assurance of redemption (Chap. 43).

In his visions of the new temple, he again provides a new salvation symbol, for the presence of the new temple is pertinent to the restoration of the covenant relationship. Then the water from the side of the temple — a sign of great fruitfulness and life to a water starved people — provides a rich concluding redemptive image. The Church was so impressed by this image that she incorporated it into her Easter liturgy in the hymn, *Vidi Aquam*.

The new catechesis partakes of the joy of the good news, hence emphasizes redemption. It would be foolish never to talk about sin, just as it would be unrealistic only to speak of redemption. Both are needed. Prophetic witness demands frowns and smiles, condemnation and inspiring proclamation, for we have to deal with sinful people who need the invitation to repent and be saved.

The prophets who looked up to heaven saw a covenant God, His cosmic glory, the majesty of the Church, the foundation of Christian hope. This came to them in terms of preexistent sky figures, chariots aflame, and whirling suns, burning coals, boiling pots, iron pillars, and dry bones. They had to eat books, sit in dungeons, be mocked at the stocks, and walk by strange rivers. In all this they witnessed God as the totally other, announced His voice, proclaimed His purity and holiness, told of the divine anger against sin and His mercy for the sinner, lived by the word of the cross and polarized their audiences into the saved and the judged.

They are fearless though sensitive, aristocratic but with empathy for the downtrodden, sometimes grumpy but never totally at a loss for compassion. Catechists are descendants of the prophets, exercising a similar ministry, sharing in a like need to challenge and protest, entrusted with God's hallowed message, prone to the same human weaknesses, exalted by a comparable inner light.

Thus is the distinguished vocation of the catechist viewed in the light of the biblical perspective. Charismatic prophecy cools from time to time in the Church, either because there is not so great a need, or because the weight of the establishment cannot loosen enough to permit such spontaneity. But Christ has sent His witness to the Church. It is His Holy Spirit who is stronger than the weight of human traditions, mightier than the crust of cultural overlay, triumphant over every effort to stifle His voice. A golden age of prophecy dawns today in our Church, and catechists are the privileged bearers of this new flame. They will shake the foundations, not to destroy the ancient Church, but to readjust its bones to fit the clothes of a new generation. These are brave new men for a brave new world, firmed and strengthened by a mysterious power from above, hardened by an uncompromising personal conviction, caught up in a vision of Christ, risen and triumphant. They love the world. The world may, as always, hate them and stone them, and live on to build a lasting memorial in their honor.

Chapter 15 ❦ A Theology of Proclamation

Catechetics is not scientific theology. It is distinct from, but not opposed to, scientific theology. By scientific theology I mean the application of a structured formal philosophy to the data of revelation for the purpose of organizing that data into conceptual patterns meaningful to the age. For most of us this generally means using the *philosophia perennis* to penetrate and organize revealed data. This is usually called speculative theology in the absolute sense. It is a necessary postulate of a living Church contemplating its divine inheritance for the purpose of a deeper knowledge of God, self, and its missionary destiny.

Catechetics is a theology of recital. It deals not only with God's revelation of Himself, but attempts to imitate as closely as possible the mode of the divine Self-disclosure. God has willed to reveal Himself by words and deeds in concrete historical situations. By these words and deeds God formed a Church which would both remember what He has said and done, and experience the effect of His word and action as salvation event. To each generation of Christians the Church proclaims the words and deeds of God. This is a theology of recital or proclamation about God's workings within the course of nature and history. The purpose of this recital is to unveil God's saving power in order to elicit surrender from the listener, a commitment of faith. Contemporary religious language terms this proclamation the "kerygma."

Many today raise questions about the philosophical under-pinnings of this theology of recital. They ask whether this theology may not be opposed to rational endeavor. Does it deny the validity of the old adage, *fides quaerens intellectum?* Is it simply a *fides quaerens fidem?* Isn't there a tone of anti-intellectualism about it? Or does it rest on the more neutral ground of indifference to the powers of rational procedure? If, by philosophical underpinnings, formal philos-ophy is meant, then I would deny its necessity for the cate-chist. *De facto,* there are almost three hundred thousand catechists in the United States, who can hardly be expected to have a grasp of formal philosophy. Furthermore, millions of Catholics sit in the pews every Sunday, devoid of the privilege of a bachelor's degree in philosophy. Only a small group of America's forty-some million Catholics have a mas-tery of a structured philosophy.

All this does not imply that catechetics rejects the influ-ence of formal philosophy, or that it is not in any way influ-enced by rational activity. A theology of recital does not mean a bare-bones mechanical announcement of the data of the Bible. Obviously the catechist is going to use and organize the material within the framework of some kind of thought pattern. There is no absolute absence of speculation. His philosophy is a loyal obedience and openness to the word. The catechist employs his intelligence to discover the method of the divine Self-disclosure, to imitate that method, and to distribute the elements in a meaningful way. He uses his reason to uncover the dynamics of the message and to ar-range it in an orderly fashion in accord with the receptivity of the students.

Any time that a reasonable man goes beyond physical data to make some sort of judgment, he enters the realm of phi-losophy. Any time he searches for ultimates and principles he is acting philosophically. (I bypass here the situation of mathematics.) I would want catechists to consider philosophy in its widest possible sense. Philosophy is not just systems.

It is also any act of the human intelligence transcending merely brute facts and surfacing to judgments about them. Any moment a man begins to think, he begins to philosophize. Practically no man acts without some kind of philosophy. For the common man it is called common sense.

Another objection has been raised. Is not the emphasis on paradox, inherent in every Christian mystery, a sort of obscurantism suppressing reason? Quite the opposite. Perhaps nothing stimulates the efforts of reason more than encounter with the paradox. It is precisely the paradox which gives the thrust to the *fides quaerens intellectum*. The refusal to face the paradox robs Christianity of its dynamism. Remove the paradox and you have stilled the voice of Christian inquiry. True, many feel uncomfortable with the tension of the paradox, but those who want a tensionless Christianity will reduce it to a sterile exercise in rote memory. The genuine scientific, speculative theologian, carefully sorting out all his ideas, polishing and rubbing them to shiny clarity, must always return with his findings to the arena of mystery and paradox. It was because theologians were forgetting this that Scheeben wrote his monumental work, *Mysteries of Christianity*. Whether you are a catechist or a theologian you must face the paradox of Christianity.

A theology of recital does not need to disparage philosophical theology in order to feel secure. The patient work of speculative theologians is one of the precious quarries which every sincere catechist must mine. Flippancies abound today about Thomism and the tyrannies of the scholastics, but I feel this is not only an irreverent lack of historical gratitude but a crass case of intellectual dishonesty. Of course alternate modes of thinking more congenial to the postscientific mind must be allowed to speak with dignity and be given a hearing by the critical minds of the intellectual community, but this is no invitation to cashier centuries of profound thinking and time-tested insights. Cults of existentialism and phenomenology lisp the more limply as long as they substitute leers for unfettered self-appraisal, and the back of the hand for parental philosophical systems while innocently and glibly feathering their own nests. Catechesis which is the joyous product of a positivist movement in modern philosophy and theology can hardly lift its head proudly if it insists on joining the chorus of nagging negativists.

At this point it may not be clear as to just where I stand. I hold that catechesis should be a theology of recital and that it should benefit from the insights of philosophical theology whether that be of the contemporary existential school or the revered expositions of the past. I do not feel it is necessary to outlaw old modes of thinking in order to swear allegiance to a present wind of doctrine. At the same time, I do feel it is legitimate to reject previous theological accommodations and catechetical methods which have been proven inadequate for our times by experts whose integrity and faithfulness to truth win a fair hearing in the Church of today.

I opt, then, for a catechesis which is a theology of proclamation. Such a catechesis assimilates the literary and pedagogical categories of the Bible. The pedagogy of Scripture is simple. Some religious message is stated, and then followed by a series of stories or parables or poetic apparatus to illustrate the meaning and quality of the message. Take, for example, the Book of Judges. The message is that when Israel sinned, God handed them over to their enemies, and after this sorrow the people of God repented and cried to God for mercy. In response to their plea He raises up a savior figure. The stories of Othoniel, Ehud, Deborah, Gideon, Jeptha, and Samson are sagas which picture the meaning of the message and define its quality. Of course, many subsidiary messages may be adduced from each of the tales, but the main principle must be kept in mind: the Bible states the message and then explains it with images.

The Bible has an interesting way of teaching paradox. We tend to conceptualize the paradox and consciously experience the tension. The biblical method is less self conscious, pre-

ferring to lay the apparent contradictions side by side. Again
Judges is a good example. The book has three stories that
have no relation directly to the message mentioned above.
The tale of Abimelech who attempts to establish a monarchy
at Shechem, and the stories about the civil strife surround-
ing the tribes of Dan and Benjamin. The rubric for these
three narratives is: "There was no king over Israel." The king
symbolizes the organization of the nation and hence their
defense against chaos. But the stories of the Judges illustrate
the value of charismatic leaders, filled with God's spirit, and
reminding the nation that only God can be the real king.
Judges are emblems of the rule of the *spirit*; kings are signs
of the *law*.

Instead of coming right out and saying, as we would, that
the necessary legalism of an organization must be counter-
balanced by the creative freedom of charism, the Bible inter-
weaves the two messages, with their corresponding images,
and by existential contrast puts the point across. The nos-
talgic accounts of the heroic exploits of the freewheeling
charismatics are balanced by the chastening stories of bar-
barism in a land infested with banditry and internal conflict.
The methodology of Scripture does not nag the reader with
message, but charms his imagination with imagery through
the pedagogy of proposition and picture.

Take the example of covenant and law. The basic idea in
covenant is relation in which God and His people are united
in love. All the codes which follow are not so much lists of
laws as they are symbolic stories which illustrate the quality
of the relation between God and the people. The law codes
are not indices of abstract legal norms, but case histories
which remind the people of the style that must regulate their
love response to God. It is the same in the new covenant.
Jesus announced only one commandment, namely, to love as
He has loved. This is the message. The long list of short-form
parables in Matthew's Sermon on the Mount is a series of
memorable images which body out the quality of the love

Christians must have. Theology of proclamation says, "Document your message with image."

This should be a consolation to catechists who may wonder how to imitate the pedagogy of Scripture and how to keep young minds interested in religion. Everyone knows that all the world loves a story. A catechesis which stems from the spirit and method of the Bible will not forget this point. Even the prophetical books, which seem the least storylike of the biblical narratives, are in reality packed with parables, historical references, and abundant poetic metaphors. If a catechist wanted to know how to teach the evil of dictators, let him use Isaiah's famed taunt song against the king of Babylon (cf. Chap. 14).

Such a catechesis has a fundamental appeal to the majority of men. Our present culture is largely structured by the image industries which foster and sometimes exploit the natural imaginative quality of the human mind. I can regret the abuse while noting the value of realizing the communication potency of the image. Some thoughtful men today are even talking in terms of a theology of the imagination. Our image-laden population must not be considered an obstacle to overcome but a valid stratum for incarnation. The theology of proclamation with its message-image dynamics is an adequate starting point not only for pedagogy but also for the process of incorporation into Christ.

Index